Enjoy the Cooler

DAMN GOOD
CHINESE FOOD

Dumplings, Egg Rolls, Bao Buns, Sesame Noodles, Roast Duck, Fried Rice, and More

50 RECIPES INSPIRED BY LIFE IN CHINATOWN

Chris Cheung
Foreword by Maneet Chauhan

Skyhorse Publishing

Skyhorse Publishing books may be purchased in bulk at special discounts for sales promotion, corporate gifts, fund-raising, or educational purposes. Special editions can also be created to specifications. For details, contact the Special Sales Department, Skyhorse Publishing, 307 West 36th Street, 11th Floor, New York, NY 10018 or info@skyhorsepublishing.com.

Skyhorse® and Skyhorse Publishing® are registered trademarks of Skyhorse Publishing, Inc.®, a Delaware corporation.

Visit our website at www.skyhorsepublishing.com.

10 9 8 7 6 5 4 3 2 1

Library of Congress Control Number: 2021913168

Cover design by Kai Texel
Cover and interior photography by Alan Battman

Author photograph on page 182 by Leslie Brienza

ISBN: 978-1-5107-5812-4
eISBN: 978-1-5107-7025-6

Printed in China

This book is dedicated to every Chinese family who struggled, strived, and kicked ass here in America.

CONTENTS

A NOTE ON LANGUAGE

For those who see different English spellings of many Chinese words within this book and wonder why, the reason is complicated: Chinese is written in characters and does not follow the Western alphabet, therefore many words were translated loosely, especially by Chinese restaurateurs in the late nineteenth century and early twentieth century as they named their new dishes to serve America their first tastes of Chinese food.

Since Chinese has different dialects, many words have been spelled in different ways to reflect those dialects.

Separately, multiple systems were created to teach and translate Chinese characters into the English alphabet, therefore many words are spelled differently depending on the system.

Most of the words and translations, to the best of my knowledge, are of Cantonese origin, and are how I grew up spelling and speaking them.

A NOTE FROM THE AUTHOR

Whether you are an experienced cook or chef, or know nothing about cooking or Chinese food, if you are planning to make these dishes, plan on making each several times. Get to know the dish, the ingredients, and the techniques. Make mistakes, and then correct them. Don't worry about exact measurements and precise cuts; use that time to enjoy the process of melding flavors and creating texture. Get used to the way your cleaver feels, taste the soy sauce, taste the marinades, taste everything as you go.

Even the most seasoned chefs refine their dishes, and we do it by repetition and trial and error. That is where you will learn great cooking. Many of the ingredients in this book may be new to you, but embrace them and learn their value to this cuisine, and soon you will begin to understand how remarkable and revered the Chinese culinary world truly is. I started learning how to cook by simply figuring out how to get a fish out of a steamer without spilling any sauce.

Fall in love making these dishes; fall in love eating them. The order is up to you.

FOREWORD

There are few people who leave a lasting impression on you—not only by the way they cook and their dedication to their craft, but also how proudly and passionately they represent their heritage. Chef Chris Cheung is one such person. His passion, his humility, his skill, and his knowledge are all apparent in his various endeavors.

With a love for Chinese ingredients, techniques, and flavors, Chris has rapidly established himself as one of the leading authorities on Chinese cuisine in the United States. Because of his in-depth knowledge of Chinese food and culture, he has been invited frequently to speak and to appear on popular television shows, such as *Anthony Bourdain's No Reservations* and as a judge on Food Network's *Chopped*.

Over the course of his career, Chris has opened some of the most exciting concept restaurants with deliciously addictive foods, one of which happens to be an amazing Nashville-based concept called Tánsuǒ, which we partnered together in opening. I was fortunate to have first met him a few years back when we were doing a media campaign together. I remember being so impressed with the flavors that he created.

We had an instant connection and quickly formed mutual respect for one another.

One of my fondest memories of Chris is cooking with him. I can close my eyes and see him making his iconic scallion pancakes with such intensity and care, or creasing those perfect folds on his divine dry-aged beef dumplings. That, to me, spoke volumes of Chris as a chef—the respect he showed the ingredients, the care and love he gave the technique, the thoughtfulness that he showed the dish. That's what makes him such a respected chef.

Chris grew up in Chinatown surrounded by its amazing history, sounds, and tastes, in a culture created by immigrants who came to the US to make a better life for themselves and their future generations. What they brought along with them were beautiful stories and flavors from the land they left behind.

Often have I wandered the streets, fascinated with what stories these walls and streets would tell—of people and food, of heritage and progress, of evolution and roots, of laughter and, at times, tears. Through his food, Chris pulls back the curtains for us and provides a generous glimpse of those wonderfully rich stories.

With this book, you will feel like you are walking these streets with him, or even sitting at his childhood dining room table when his mom walks in with the white cake box filled with treasures like roast pork buns, shumai dumplings, and sesame balls with red bean. He brings us back to the forgotten and long-gone teashops and restaurants that served his favorite snacks by recreating them in this book.

In addition to these recipes, Chris touches on important time-honored techniques like dumpling folding and the love of preserved foods, which have been an integral part of Chinese cooking for centuries.

The recipes and techniques in this book are undoubtedly authentic, but also approachable and delicious. These dishes will excite you and quickly become family favorites. I am ready to dive into these mouthwatering recipes and look forward to cooking up a delicious, Chris-inspired storm in my own kitchen!

—**Maneet Chauhan**, judge on *Chopped*, winner of *Tournament of Champions II*, and author of *Chaat*

INTRODUCTION

STORIES OF CHINATOWN SNACKS

Mott Street, New York City, in the late 1970s—disco, gangsters, Cadillacs, and damn good Chinese food.

Like most chefs, my inspiration comes from remembering the joys of eating great things as a kid. Of course, those memories are always associated with something: whether it's your grandmother or just a memory of a summer gone by. Mine is the neighborhood I grew up in: Chinatown.

Back in the day, teahouses were on every street—little shops with round stools and Formica counters, like a Chinese-style Chock Full o' Nuts. Under the crackling fluorescent lights were tables and booths all set with a sugar pourer and metal cans filled with spoons, forks, and chopsticks. An old man in a gray waiter's jacket with a cigarette hanging from his mouth stood behind the counter taking orders.

The stuff behind that counter was magic. He was the keeper of that stuff. He would take these little snacks and place them in a cake box (you know, with the big flaps that never behave once you open them). He would then tie the box with a red-and-white string that came from some contraption (that

somehow also helped tie the boxes), effortlessly twirling the slack over each side into a neat bow. He could simultaneously answer the old black rotary phone and point randomly at the first customer waiting to catch his eye and fill both orders in seconds while also checking his OTB ticket. You would point to the sesame balls, rice rolls, egg tarts, and he would toss them into wax paper bags and into the box they would go.

It was this great food that fueled Chinatown. We were all poor—some of the first of us that made it here survived famine in China and lived through the Great Depression in America. That's pretty much my grandparents' story. They worked hard, over twelve hours a day—my grandmother at the sweatshop, sewing shirts for a penny a button; my grandfather as a restaurant worker. When you live like that, you live for your family. When you work like that, you want to eat well. Chinatown was lucky to have great food as one of its true treasures.

I'll always remember when my mom would come home on a Sunday afternoon with that box tied together with the red-and-white string. She would place it on the kitchen table, cut the string, and the box would collapse ever so slightly as the steam released all the aromas into the room and into our noses. Everyone had a favorite. Mine were the roast pork buns, the sesame balls filled with red bean, and—of course—the dumplings.

The Magic of *Har Gow*

My love of dumplings started as soon as I could eat them. I was eight years old, and there was a little hole-in-the-wall restaurant downstairs from my grandmother's apartment. Sometimes, when I was hungry and well-behaved she would give me a buck to go down and get an order of *har gow* (shrimp dumplings).

When I think about those days, I can still taste those dumplings. I'm sure part of it was the reward factor, but mostly it was because they were among the best I've ever had. Even though I was more famished than well-behaved, I usually found a way to get my hands on those freshly steamed, silky-skinned shrimp that melted in your mouth. They served them in a paper boat and I just ate them up—one, two, three, four, always wishing I had more.

Later on, as a teenager, I would have to pass through Chinatown street gangs just to enjoy my favorite snacks. You realize how much you love this food when you risk street fighting with gangsters to get those dumplings.

I didn't know it at the time, but these would be memories I would hold on to throughout my cooking career. The magic of these dumplings would inspire me as a chef and influence how I cooked. I try to connect with those I'm cooking for, and bring them back to their own fond memories as a kid eating something that they will never forget and always cherish.

Preservation

There was nothing better as a kid growing up in Chinatown than going to the movies. There were three theaters: Music Palace, Sun Sing, and Pagoda. They showed all those Hong Kong films like *The Shao Lin Temple*, *The 5 Deadly Venoms*, and all the first-run kung fu flicks.

The appeal to us, as kids, was that the theaters were haunted. They even took out the seats in the first row, leaving the empty frames for the ghosts to "sit" and watch the movies with the rest of us, so naturally that was where we used to hang out.

The snacks still stand out in my mind. Yes, there was popcorn, but this was old-school Chinatown! Our favorite munchies at the movies were preserved, salted cuttlefish and Malaysian beef jerky. You would buy them right at the snack counter, one bag of each and a soda. No Buncha Crunch or Sour Patch Kids here!

Many of you, I know, are saying: "Really? Who eats dried beef and seafood at the movies?" You have to understand the obsession Chinese people have for packaged preserved food. There are entire sections at the Chinese supermarket devoted to these snacks. Family members will bring back a dedicated suitcase of the stuff from their hometowns in China. (TSA officers know better than most people how much we love our snacks.)

Chinese people take great pride in their preserved food, as they have been practicing preserving techniques for thousands of years. Let's put it this way: in China—way, way back in the day—if you weren't preserving food, when winter came, you died of starvation.

Now, centuries later, we have a taste for these foods that's in our blood. There is an invisible river of salt and sugar running through the bodies of all Chinese people. It's not necessarily about survival anymore. The craving for seafood, meats, eggs, vegetables—and pretty much anything that can be preserved—is ingrained in our DNA.

In China today, on the rooftops and in the courtyards, people still just randomly hang fish to dry in the sun. A stroll around any Chinese market will display thousand-year eggs, dried mushrooms of all kinds, sea cucumbers, and even three-foot preserved squids!

There is not a more important type of food in Chinese culture than what we can preserve. Whether it's eating dried cuttlefish at the movies or smuggling suitcases of it out of China, there's no denying that this is a serious part of our diet and livelihood.

Chinatown Forever

Chinatown tends to change slowly, but it is changing. Today, most of those teahouses have closed, along with the theaters. Now there are bubble tea shops, karaoke bars, huge markets, and food courts.

I have seen our community grow, and experienced the pains and joys of the Chinese American journey. It's a place where we all came together to survive, to succeed, and to make our contribution to American culture.

The one constant is Chinese people love their food. We love cooking and we love eating. I want to share with you the connections this cuisine has to Chinese culture and people in America.

CHAPTER 1

THE MARKET

The market is the most important place in Chinatown. All great things come from there and everyone—I mean, *everyone*—goes there. New York City's Chinatown is actually just one big market from Mulberry Street to East Broadway. The streets are filled with small little stalls and stores each with their own specialty.

Explore and find the best vendors selling fruit at the base of the Manhattan Bridge. Judge for yourself if that store on Mott Street has the tastiest tofu. Find the fresh rice noodles in Chatham Square, and search for the best Chinese sausages on Hester Street.

Make a point to find places you love, and remember them forever. Then head out to Brooklyn and check out what they got, or take a trip to Flushing, Queens. You will find it's a different world out there and well worth the trip.

If you aren't in New York City, visit a Chinatown nearest to you and spend the day wandering around. Find every place you can that has high-quality products.

The Chinese Supermarket

In every Chinatown, you'll typically find a big Chinese supermarket. They are massive stores with thousands of things to buy and eat. They have a culture all their own and can be almost overwhelming. But embrace this place, because all the cooking begins here. The international section at Key Foods just ain't gonna cut it. To know the Chinese market is to know Chinese food.

At the market you will find the most important group of people in Chinatown: little old Chinese ladies. True Chinese food was derived through peasant food, and was cloned when it was introduced to America by these ladies. They come at you—short, cute, and feisty.

A little old Chinese lady once smacked me in the back of my head for moving her shopping cart. I must have gotten in her way in a narrow supermarket aisle, and she wasn't going to let me slip by without expressing her disapproval. They can be truly gangsta at times!

All shopping cart turf wars aside, I love these ladies. My grandmother was one. My mother, who is now a grandmother, is one.

These ladies make the dumplings at my restaurant, East Wind Snack Shop. You see them on the subway all toting their little red plastic bags, always filled with goodies they bought at the Chinatown markets as they make their way home to cook for all of us. You want to know what traditional and authentic Chinese food is? If a little old Chinese lady likes it, it's authentic.

They are old-school. All they eat and cook is Chinese food. They are the true carriers of the torch in Chinese cooking. They don't get Michelin stars. They don't aspire to be Food Network celebrities. They just know how to cook, and have fed all of Chinatown for the past hundred years. Having your grandmother cook you the food she ate as a little kid in China becomes part of you, just as it is a part of her and all of the family. It's the true spirit of the cuisine.

So, when you see these ladies in the market, listen as they judge the produce. Look at the sauces they are buying. Admire how they command the butcher to cut their order to their specifications. And try not to get in their way.

TIPS FOR NAVIGATING THE CHINESE SUPERMARKET

- Choose your market wisely. Notice how the purveyors take care of and display the vegetables. They'd better be well-trimmed, all brightly colored and robust, and stacked up high and neat.

- Yes, the crabs are alive in that barrel, as are the lobsters in the tanks. So are the frogs and turtles. If they aren't alive, don't buy them. It's not a dead pet sale. The crabs and lobsters go home with you alive, but the frogs and turtles can be given to the fishmonger to be butchered and cleaned properly for you.

- Enjoy all the different dialects and languages that aren't English. Cantonese used to be the common language, but now it's mostly Mandarin, especially in Queens, and maybe some Fujianese. There can be lots of yelling, but just embrace it. These are the natural sounds of being in the Chinese market.

- In the Chinese supermarket, the aisles are narrow, and no one really rushes to move aside with their carts. They will eventually, but it's like driving behind an Uber—you know he ain't pulling over, he is just going to stop right in the middle of the road to unload his passengers while you wait.

- There is no line or take-a-number at the butcher (or any of the sections) except at the register when you pay. You just have to catch their eye. If you are not assertive, a little old Chinese lady will cut you, and having shown weakness, three more people will attempt to steal your turn. You could be there forever.

- In New York, it's fun to shop at the Chinese markets as a special trip, but if you find yourself frequenting the markets, parking will inevitably become a factor. Luckily, most of the big markets will have a parking lot. It's very convenient to park and load all your groceries into the car at one time.

- In many cities, there isn't any Chinatown, but where there is an Asian community, there will be an Asian market for your shopping needs. At the very least there are online sources for many essential products that you may not find at your local grocery store. Worst case, you can always check on Amazon.

AMAZING INGREDIENTS YOU CAN BUY AT THE CHINESE SUPERMARKET

Fresh Produce

This is a big section. There are varieties of fruits and vegetables here you won't find anywhere else. Like I said in the market tips section, pay attention to how they treat and display their greens. Vegetables in the market are sold at high volumes and that means they are always fresh. Price is dictated by the volume, so they are also cheap. Outside of New York City, there are many farms that exist just to supply Chinatown. The produce is local, but it is not the focus like it is at farmer's markets. It's more about providing delicious, affordable food for your family.

I find more inspiration here to cook than any trip to the Greenmarkets. Don't get me wrong, I love the Greenmarket, but I once spent twenty bucks on two daikon radishes and two heads of garlic. Do you know how many bags of delicious greens you can get for twenty bucks at the Chinese market?

You also have to get up early to get the good stuff at the Greenmarkets. I'm a chef who works past midnight, so waltzing into the Chinese market at noon and still having choice picks works well for me.

Of course, you will find onions, scallions, ginger, carrots, garlic, and all the essential vegetables and aromatics for Chinese cooking. You can pick oranges, apples, and grapes, depending on the season. Bok choy, Chinese celery, bitter melon, lotus root, Chinese broccoli, choy sum, yu choy, fuzzy melon, winter melon, water spinach, snow pea shoots, and long beans will all be available to you. You will also find dragon fruit, lychees, longans, mangosteens, and if you are lucky (or unlucky, depending on your taste),

durian. If you don't know what durian is, then that is yet another reason to check out the Chinese market.

One of my favorite vegetables to cook is bok choy. There are so many varieties, ranging from baby shoots to big heads of the stuff. They can be mostly white with a touch of green, or vice versa. The baby shoots you can just clean and cook as they are. The larger heads you have to cut down, cut off the heart, wash, and then cook. There is a butter-like essence that comes out when you stir-fry them. With oil, garlic, ginger, Shaoxing (Also known as "Shao Hsing") wine, soy sauce, and a little sauté skill, you have your first Chinese vegetable dish!

The Fishmonger

Live fish and seafood are the benchmarks of Chinese cuisine. It's a characteristic of both home and restaurant cooking, which means that it's a way of life, not just a culinary nugget that many would stick their chest out just to show off. Whether it's at home or at a restaurant, we always demand the freshest fish and seafood possible. Every dish is judged in this regard first, before flavor, creativity, or authenticity.

You will never see a better collection of live seafood than in the Chinese supermarket. It is an aquarium for the hungry. In the tanks, you will see swimming striped bass, black bass, and snapper in season, as well as snakefish and eel. Check out the next tank showcasing lobster, Dungeness crabs, and sweet shrimp.

I always feel sorry for the frogs and turtles. They are alive, but always seem to sit in the tank, water only halfway up their green little bodies, motionless as if they are hypnotized, waiting to be soup.

In half-cut barrels right in front you can pick blue crabs. Please note: They can get feisty. The fishmongers sell them without rubber bands on the claws, so occasionally one will try to escape.

These crabs always amazed me as a kid, seeing hundreds of them just snapping and crawling. The fishmonger would use these long tongs to snatch 'em up and put them in a paper bag for us to bring home and enjoy.

They looked even better as they were being readied to cook. My grandmother would empty them into the sink to wash, and then would remove the top shell before chopping them all in half to reveal the eggs and guts—you know, all the good stuff.

Then she'd heat up the wok. After shaking those crabs in egg, scallion, and ginger with a touch of ground pork, she'd finish it off with some soy sauce and fermented black beans and slide it all off into a big bowl. All you would hear for the next half hour would be the crunching of crab shells.

The Butcher

Remember my previous market tip and get to the counter, as close to the butcher as possible. Expect someone to try to order before you do. Don't be shy. Tell the butcher what you want. Be careful, though: It can be like Black Friday at the mall—you could get trampled for three-dollar-a-pound pork belly!

The meat of choice in Chinese cuisine is pork. It is the king of meats. Everything revolves around it.

We use almost every part of the pig when we cook. The nose, the hocks, and pretty much everything in between. You can even get a base stock through simmering the bones and cooking fat from the lard.

The most popular cuts are the belly and the butt. Some cuts are undeniably best for Chinese barbecue; others show off their greatness through slow-cooking and stews.

If you are going to make dumplings without hand-chopping the meat, you will need ground pork from the Chinese market. Leaner cuts like pork chops and tenderloin are available for all of your cooking needs.

If beef is what you want to cook, try the short rib or even oxtail. In the poultry section, you can find many varieties of birds sitting side by side: wild duck, black chicken, partridge, and quail. These are the types of ingredients that will bring out the inner chef in all of us.

You may want to look around the butcher's case a bit to figure out what you want. Yes, there are chicken breasts and flank steak, but try the tripe, the duck's tongue, or even the chicken feet. Any part of the pig or cow you can think of, the Chinese supermarket will have it and the butcher will cut it to order.

Just accept this fact going into it: There isn't heritage duroc pork. No small farm grass-fed beef. Nothing is organic. It's meat for the working class. Many Chinese dishes use cuts of meats that are slow-cooked, which tend to be less expensive but are just as tasty because they draw their flavor from the intensity of cooking.

For the lower-quality cuts that require quick cooking, there are techniques like marinating and velveting that can elevate the meats in many dishes. These methods are explained on pages 70–71 and are used throughout the book.

The Preserved Food Section

Preserved foods in Chinese cooking are next level. There are so many types of preserved foods that you will actually find them all around the market, not just in one section. Scattered throughout its magical aisles are salted fish, Chinese sausage, Chinese bacon, beef jerky, dried shrimp, dried scallops, sea cucumber, dozens of different types of mushrooms—the list goes on and on. These ingredients are used for cooking and are eaten as snacks in the home.

Chinese foodies are addicted to hundred-year-old eggs. You can eat them plain or with rice. Are they really aged for a hundred years? No, they are made by burying the eggs in a special mix of minerals and salt for up to three months. These eggs yield a solid black egg white and the yolk is creamy; they look like a Bizarro egg and are among the most interesting foods in the world.

Every culture has its charcuterie and Chinese culture is no exception. *Lap Cheong* (Chinese sausage) and *Lap Yuk* (Chinese bacon) are sun-dried preserved meats that are staples in Chinese cooking. You will see them on display, hanging like the salami at Katz's Deli, and they are just as good. Also on display, in bins and packages and hanging all around the market, is all the dried preserved seafood—perfect for cool Instagram pics and then for dinner.

The Sauce and Seasoning Aisle

Sauces and seasonings have their own dedicated sections and aisles in the market. X/O sauce, black bean garlic sauce, oyster sauce, hoisin sauce, and chili sauce can all be found there. There will be things from every corner of Asia, not just China.

Don't like chili-garlic sauce? Try Lao Gan Ma, which is peanut chili oil with the little old Chinese lady on the label. Want BBQ sauce? Try satay sauce or just stick to plain hoisin.

It can be a bit confusing to decide which ones are right for you. Lee Kum Kee is a very popular company that covers a lot of the bases and must-have sauces in the Chinese pantry. Try some of those and see which you like best. If you want to cook proper Chinese food, you will need a basic combination of condiments in your pantry.

Soy Sauce

First and foremost, you will need to try out and pick a soy sauce. This is an absolute necessity in Chinese cooking. I cannot stress enough the importance of having a high-quality soy sauce to work with since it's used in so many recipes.

Some soy sauces are stronger than others; some are sweet or seasoned. For most cooking, you will need a thin and dark soy. Each should have depth, not just a salt hit. You should taste a touch of the fermentation, and both should have a deep aroma with a subtle note of earthiness. You will sense the salinity no matter what soy you are trying, but as you become more familiar with each sauce, you will be able to pick out the different flavors like a connoisseur can with a fine wine.

Thin soy is perfect to finish a stir-fry; sweet soy is divine in a dipping sauce; dark soy is great for a marinade. A squirt of soy on rice makes a delicious lunch if you are busy or broke.

For the majority of dishes in Chinese cuisine, soy sauce is used instead of salt. I know for many Western cooks it's strange to have to hold back from sprinkling salt on every dish before being served, but that is traditional in Chinese cooking. Drop the salt and come over to the dark side. Learn how to utilize it and love it or you will never cook Chinese food properly.

Oyster Sauce

According to food legend, years ago, there was a little stall in China that sold oysters. One day, the owner left his pot on with simmering oysters and forgot that it was cooking. When he noticed the potent smell coming from the pot, he lifted the lid and saw that the oysters had cooked into a thick brown sauce. It turned out to be a million-dollar mistake as he went on to found Lee Kum Kee, one of the top condiment companies in the Chinese food industry today.

Oyster sauce is a bomb of savory flavor that adds a dark, lush, and exceptionally rich glaze to Chinese sauces. This essential condiment provides recipes with depth, flavor, and that extra something that makes them sing. It plays a large part in stir-fried dishes, and is used in dozens, if not hundreds, of dishes in the Chinese kitchen, including so many Chinese classics. Whether using it to layer a sauce or as a straight condiment on sautéed Chinese broccoli, oyster sauce can round out almost any savory dish.

It is truly an enricher, though, as any condensed seafood base would be. Try cooking these dishes without oyster sauce and you will taste a big difference, as if the soy sauce is lonely without it. Don't cook lonely food. A world without oyster sauce is like a world without Classic Coke, and who would want that?

Shaoxing Wine

There is something about cooking with wine no matter where you are from. Shaoxing wine (also spelled "Shao Hsing") is used more frequently in cooking north of Hong Kong, but it is a great thing to have in any Chinese pantry. It takes its name from the province where they make the wine, and most bottles are labeled SHAOXING or SHAO HSING for easy identification.

When I cooked in China, we had Shaoxing wine that came in plastic bags, where you cut the corner, poured it into the wok, and drank the rest. In China it's a "get-drunk-while-you-are-cooking" type of wine. We cook with wine in the Shanghai region just as much as the French do.

There is something sublime when the wine hits a hot wok sizzling with ginger and garlic. The steam rises into the air and the mixture gives off its heavenly aroma. Then you add some oyster and soy sauce, and *poof*! You have the base for over a hundred stir-fry recipes.

Oils

Sesame oil is not primarily used for cooking like vegetable or olive oil. It is more of a flavoring agent used in sauces and marinades. The strong flavor is vital in many dishes. It works great as a nutty, earthy element in dipping sauces. One ancient Chinese technique is to heat sesame oil until its smoking point, and then add it to various sauces.

We typically use a lot of peanut oil in stir-fry cooking for its flavor, but it has been less popular recently due to allergic reactions, so I use mostly vegetable oil for the recipes in this book.

Sugar and Spices

At the market you can explore the many types of seasonings that stock the pantries of the Chinese household. It can be a little overwhelming, so focus on these first:

Chinese sugar is a more flavorful alternative to plain white sugar. It comes in bars that you can crush or break. Keep in mind you will need to have some white granulated sugar on hand as well.

Chinese five-spice powder is also a popular seasoning mix, which typically consists of pepper, star anise, cumin, clove, and cinnamon. It's used for BBQed meats, in many marinades, and as a salt to flavor fried foods.

You typically will be able to find all of these in the spice, tea, and seasoning aisle (or right within the sauce aisle). This section contains all the various powders, flours, spices, starches, and all the different kinds of MSG.

MSG

OK, MSG. It is the one ingredient in Chinese cooking that divides people here in America. In China, the supermarkets have an entire aisle devoted to the many varieties. They even sell it by the barrel. In Chinese supermarkets, so many boxes of it are stacked like the cereal aisles at your local grocery store.

I chose to leave MSG in my recipes because it is necessary to yield the traditional taste of some classic dishes. It's celebrated and widely used like many other food seasonings, yet it still for some reason has a negative stigma attached to it.

I'm not saying it's healthy for you, but salt can give you high blood pressure, sugar and diabetes are linked, and the caffeine in coffee is an addictive stimulant. Foods like butter and other oils are high in fat and can lead to obesity and heart disease. They are all accepted in moderation and none of these foods are negatively associated with a particular group of people, but MSG is, which begs the question: why?

My friend, the late great Anthony Bourdain, called racism on this and I have to agree with him. I have professionally cooked Japanese food, Thai food, and American food, and MSG was used in all of these kitchens, but I have only ever seen the request, "please, no MSG" when cooking at a Chinese restaurant. I feel the message they are trying to send is that Chinese people are trying to make you sick through their food. This is not the only shot of racism pointed at us. It starts with MSG and goes to so many other dark places.

There are many people in the food industry who cook Chinese food to only elevate themselves and have no respect for the people and the culture. We have brought so many people together with our food; just look around at the diversity in any busy Chinese restaurant. Everyone is together having a great time eating Chinese food. We are here and we've paid our dues, and we ain't going away. Chinese food is forever, and yeah, we make it with MSG.

The Packaged Snacks Aisle

Like everyone, Chinese people are addicted to eating snacks. It's a global pastime. As far as I know, snacks, the couch, and the TV were all invented together at the same time like it was a package deal. A quick stop at the Chinese market and you can sit back and eat all the shrimp chips, crab crackers, dumplings, ramen noodles, and almond cookies you can handle.

As you stroll around the market, you will find countless snacks. The candy aisle is naturally a fun section. In Chinese culture, candy is a symbol of a happy life. In China, people pack little bags of candy to give out to their neighbors to celebrate marriage.

Chinese sweets, especially the packaged ones, are much different from the American kind. Not much in the way of chocolate, but it seems that market is growing a bit as of late. Different fruits, red bean, and lotus seed paste are the tastes of choice. Some will have savory ingredients mixed in which, of

course, is an acquired taste. I grew up eating salted preserved plums, Haw Flakes made from Chinese hawthorn, and White Rabbit milk candies. (The White Rabbit candies were always fun because you would eat the rice paper that wrapped the candy, and your teeth would tense a bit from all the chewing.)

The Rest of the Market

Instant ramen noodles are a great option when craving snacks—quick and easy cooking with hundreds of different flavors from all over Asia. Boil water, open packets of seasoning, add noodles, and you have a convenient and tasty snack. There is a whole dried-noodle section in the Chinese market.

American college kids have adopted it as the fuel that propels them to graduation since the low cost of the snack also helps to subsidize the cost of tuition. Without these awesome noodles we would probably be surrounded by broke, really hungry college dropouts. You are welcome, America.

Go to the perimeter of the market and typically you will find the refrigerated and freezer sections.

In the refrigerated section, you will see fresh ho fun noodles made from rice, lo mein noodles made from wheat, and everything in between. You can also treat yourself to some fresh, locally made tofu.

Frozen snacks are an option, too—everything from frozen bao buns to scallion pancakes. These snacks are always great for having around when you need a quick breakfast, or to enjoy during a movie night at home.

Of course, the thing we eat the most can be found in the front by the checkout counter in twenty-five pound bags: Rice. Jasmine rice, sticky rice, all types of grains from all over Asia.

Rice is a valuable thing. Are you familiar with the saying "finish your food because there are starving kids in China"? They were talking about all those little old Chinese ladies growing up in the famine. Rice is more than just a food; it has played a big part in all our lives, and has been at the center of Chinese cuisine for millennia.

CHAPTER 2

COOKING TOOLS AND EQUIPMENT

If you aren't familiar with Chinese culture, you will begin to notice there are some differences compared to the West. We don't have an alphabet, thirteen is not an unlucky number, and we eat using chopsticks. The food is definitely not the same, and so many of our cooking tools may be a new thing for many out there just getting started in Chinese cuisine.

It's pretty awesome to have a new world of "kitchen stuff" that you can buy and try.

While they may be new to you, many of these kitchen gadgets have been around for thousands of years.

Please respect these tools, as it can be difficult to prepare some dishes without them. The good news is that you can get familiar with the techniques of use fairly quickly and easily. They are usually all available at the big Chinese supermarket, and are reasonably inexpensive, so clear some space in your kitchen and get your chopsticks ready.

Rice Cookers

You will need something to cook rice in. Thankfully, someone invented the electric rice cooker.

When I was younger, my mom would make pork cakes and string beans with fermented tofu for dinner, and that meant food for the next day. All you had to do was click the button and the rice would steam. Just before it was done, I would add the "pork and beans" and there was an after-school meal.

Cooking rice this way is the easy way: wash the rice, add water, cover, click the button, and wait. Before this miraculous machine, you cooked rice in a pot on the stove. I know of many old-school chefs in Chinatown that still refuse to cook rice in a cooker. The grains react differently when cooking on a stovetop and absorb the water less quickly, yielding a slightly drier outer crust. Your choice, but if you go the old-school way, be careful: you have to watch it or the bottom will burn.

Most of us have gotten used to the rice cooker. You will appreciate its convenience and how well it cooks rice—how it applies a constant temperature that cooks evenly or how it can hold and keep the rice warm for hours without much change in quality. Not to mention it's easy to clean and inexpensive. Buy this and have a never-ending supply of cooked rice ready to go along with all the recipes in this book.

The Chinese Steamer

The circular steamer will enable you to cook so many things conveniently, from dumplings to whole fish. You can even cook them simultaneously since steamers have layers.

Steamers are typically made out of bamboo or aluminum. Bamboo has this retro, authentic look that is unique to any kitchen. You will need a deep pan to heat the water and to fit the bamboo layers on top. The aluminum version will last longer and is much easier to clean. Either way, make sure they are stacked evenly and check the cover for a tight seal that will ensure the best steaming results in your cooking.

Dumpling-Making Equipment

A miniature rolling pin is necessary if you want to make your own dumpling wrappers. This tool is unique for dumplings, and is smaller and thinner than a standard pastry rolling pin. I can't imagine making dumplings without this simple, yet essential tool.

If you are using dough to make dumpling wrappers, make sure you buy a bench cutter, which helps with both cutting and portioning your dough.

Additionally, you will need something to put your dumplings on as you make them. Half or quarter aluminum sheet pans are recommended.

Buy a nonstick pan with a clear cover if you want to cook potstickers, which are a style of dumpling that is cooked in water and seared to finish. I call for a clear cover to save you the effort of lifting the lid every thirty seconds to see if all the cooking water has boiled out.

Wok

Get a decent-sized wok. The most common sizes are 12 and 14 inches. You will need to season it. To do this: separate and quickly blanch approximately 8 large napa cabbage leaves. Pat the leaves dry and coat one side lightly with kosher salt. Line the wok with the leaves salt-side down. Heat the wok until it smokes, remove from heat, discard the leaves, and then wipe it all down with a towel dipped in vegetable oil.

It's also a good idea to learn the hot spots and familiarize yourself with its temperatures and how long it takes cook certain things, as it varies dramatically from normal pans.

No, you don't have to flip the wok like you see professional chefs doing on TV or in a restaurant. Use a round scoop and flat spatula to move food around as you cook. The corner of the spatula will twirl noodles around in the wok without breaking them. Use the scoop to ladle out sauces.

The Chinese Cleaver

Get used to cutting with a cleaver when cooking Chinese food. Buy a Chinese cleaver. This knife is different from a Western cleaver. It's extremely versatile and is good for more than just chopping meat. It's great for mincing vegetables. It does the heavy cutting when you need leverage. It can crush garlic with its broad side. You can chop all of your veggies and then transfer them to the plate, pan, or wok in one sweep. Plus, you'll look like a badass walking around with a big cleaver.

Other Useful Tools

There is also some specialty equipment that you will need for some of these recipes. Kitchen people are usually incredibly resourceful when faced with kitchen equipment problems; we will MacGyver anything to suit our needs. However, consider buying these tools, which will help you cook the recipes in this book with ease. I list these hoping that your kitchen already has some of the basics.

- **Meat hooks and skewers**—great for drying and cooking Chinese barbecue properly
- **Spider strainer**—a six-inch wire strainer that makes blanching, shocking, and frying very easy
- **Pastry brush**—for applying sauces or glazes evenly and sparingly
- **Whisk**—better than a spoon or fork, it mixes and helps to emulsify liquids
- **Roasting rack**—great for letting meats rest and fried foods to shed any excess oil

- **Roasting pan**—a larger pan to cook whole birds and roast meats
- **Perforated hotel pan**—a pan with holes in it needed for drying rice for fried rice and draining fillings for spring rolls and egg rolls
- **Whole and half hotel pan**—great pans for storing food
- **Mixing bowls**—aluminum bowls that make mixing dumpling fillings easy
- **Stockpots**—medium to large pots needed for making stock and congee, and for blanching and frying
- **Saucepans and sauce pots**—small to medium pots and pans that you will need to cook sauces and reduce liquids
- **Stand mixer**—electric mixer saves you time and energy when kneading dough and mixing ingredients
- **Food processor**—electric appliance great for bulk cutting of vegetables
- **Instant-read thermometer**—no better way to tell if something is done

Additional Notes on Equipment

When you begin to cook these recipes, you will need to have certain things at the ready.

You should have a stockpot filled with water for blanching, and ice in a large mixing bowl, ready for shocking.

For certain dishes, you will also need a fryer or stockpot filled with hot oil to flash-fry. This technique is explained on page 71. Two gallons of vegetable oil in a three-gallon stockpot will do for home use. You will need to use larger equipment like your wok for frying things like whole duck or chicken, so don't confuse the two, and use the wok when it is noted.

Frying is an important part of cooking in Cantonese cuisine, so get used to the technique, be safe, and be careful of any water left in the pots or on any of the equipment before frying to avoid splatter. Have a system to strain the oil, and when dirty, have a place to discard it that is environmentally compliant.

Now that you have a feel for some of the ingredients, unwrapped your new rice cooker, and have all your equipment lined up, you are ready to do some cooking.

CHAPTER 3

HOME COOKING

The Dynasty of Lost Recipes

Jo Gwan is the Chinese kitchen god. His story is a famous and tragic tale of a god who used to be mortal. His powers could enhance a home's happiness and fortune if the house was harmonious and peaceful. He could also damn a house with bad luck and misfortune if chaos and pettiness were present. An image of him would usually hang over the kitchen stove, and sometimes the inhabitants of the home would smear honey on his mouth so only sweet things could be said of the house. I have always been inspired by his image in my family's kitchen and so I want to share with you a story of Jo Gwan that I had once day-dreamed of while waiting for a pot of water to boil.

One of Jo Gwan's descendants, his great-granddaughter Gee Shee, was a caretaker of the emperor's eighth child. Eight is the luckiest of numbers in Chinese culture, and while, of course, this child was not as high-standing as the firstborn, he was special, and Gee Shee loved Little Eight like he was her own son.

One day, Gee Shee was given a great chance to impress the emperor and was bestowed the privilege of preparing a birthday dinner for Little Eight. It was to be the occasion of the year!

Many weeks were spent in preparation for the event. She researched all of the emperor's favorite dishes, shared every great dish she knew, and taught the Royal Kitchen all of Little Eight's favorite meals. She would look lovingly into his eyes, "I'll always make your favorite dishes," she promised sweetly. She put her heart and soul, sweat and tears, heaven and earth, into that party.

The mother of the emperor's ninth child did not like all the attention that was being paid to anyone that wasn't her child, especially Little Eight. In a jealous rage, she vowed to ruin the party. She was a conniving and shrewd woman, and tricked the Royal Kitchen into sabotaging the dinner and blaming the caretaker.

Thanks to the evil mother's antics, the night was a disaster and the emperor was embarrassed. Gee Shee was therefore banished from the kingdom. She was heartbroken as she looked into Little Eight's eyes for the last time, and felt shame and sorrow for breaking her promise to the boy she loved. Then, as she was led out of the city, bitterness glazed her mouth and she cursed the palace. "May no love exist in the kitchen for a hundred years!" The powers of her great-grandfather suddenly ignited and a curse spread across the land.

Without love, nothing was passed down to the next generation, and great dishes and their recipes were forever lost. Chefs seemed to lose their talent, crops never yielded their full bounty, and food everywhere just seemed a little too sour. No one ate well. This went on for many years until the great-grandson of the ninth child, Tze On, uncovered how it all happened.

Tze On was a stand-up guy, and he wanted to make things right. He gave up his title and went out in search of any remaining family of Little Eight's caretaker.

With no title or riches, he traveled the countryside, earning his keep cooking and working at many teahouses from town to town. When he reached Guangdong Province, he met a girl in one of these establishments, the owner's daughter. Tze On quickly learned the girl was sick, and it appeared that she didn't have much time left in this world. He cared for her, cooked for her, and, of course, fell in love with her.

"I'll always make your favorite dishes," he promised.

When he found out the teahouse had formerly been called Little Eight, he knew this was the family he had been looking for. Their new love broke the curse and restored the girl's health. They passed down all their recipes to their daughters, and this began a new era in Chinese cooking all over the country.

They returned love to the Chinese kitchen. However, for every dish that wasn't passed down, there was a broken heart.

Sunday Dinner

I grew up in a Toisan kitchen watching my grandmother cook for the family. You don't appreciate it as a kid, but when I think back to those days at the dinner table, sitting and waiting with chopsticks in hand, bowl of rice ready to be topped, gazing at delicious plates of food, I am now aware of how lucky I was to eat my grandma's home cooking.

She, my mom, and my aunt Sandra made miracles in that tiny kitchen. Their traditional Toisan cooking fattened me up with dishes like minced pork and salted egg, steamed fish with black bean, and string beans with preserved bean paste.

I can still see the pots simmering away on the stove. The best was lifting the cover off the pot and carefully removing the plate of fish, fighting off the steam that was shooting off the sides. The sauce that collected on the plate swirling with the natural jus

of the fish would slide off if you didn't hold it steady. They never once spilled a drop of that beautiful sauce, and that fish was always devoured as soon as it hit the table. You learn to quickly lunge for food while still trying to look like you have manners.

Being raised in a Chinese household where a lot of cooking is done bestows a level of confidence and appreciation for authenticity. The experience elevates you beyond just a passion for cooking Chinese food. It's a part of us, it helps to define us, and it's given us life.

In this chapter I will share a glimpse of that precious moment years ago, and I hope it will inspire you to cook with your family. Make these simple recipes—or the whole dinner—with pride, precision, nostalgia, history, and, of course, a big bowl of rice.

RICE

The only thing more absorbed by the Chinese body than rice is air, and maybe not even that. We can eat rice at every meal. We grind it into powder to make baked and steamed foods, dry it overnight to cook fried rice, mix it to form rice cakes, and simmer it for hours in congee.

At the dinner table, a bowl of rice, unseasoned, is the perfect canvas for culinary masterpieces. Those dishes would symbolize love, hard work, dignity, endurance, devotion, and family. In the Chinese home, you can't have those elements without rice. Let me be clear: Rice is life.

In Chinese culture, it's the first thing you learn to cook. I remember my mother showing me how to scoop the rice out of the bag with the little cup that came with the rice cooker, which is in every Chinese home.

The collection of offbeat Chinese kitchen tools includes this cup, along with kitchen scissors with which parents cut noodles, vegetables, and every other food for their toddlers; a metal rack used for steaming stuff in pots; brightly colored plastic colanders; and, of course, the big white spoon, which also comes with the rice cooker. If these items cannot be found somewhere in your kitchen, you are not allowed to be Chinese. They are prerequisites when applying for the membership card.

MAKES 6 BOWLS | PREP TIME: 3 MINUTES | COOKING TIME: 25 MINUTES

INGREDIENTS
3 cups rice (medium-long grain or jasmine rice)
3½ cups water (give or take)

Tip:
Rice can be dried and held in warehouses for months before being packed for sale and export. An important thing to note is that sometimes rice bags are labeled "new crop" or "fresh crop." In some purchasing cycles, the rice gets packed much quicker and contains more moisture. It affects cooking in one way, so make sure you add less water when cooking. At the Chinese table, there is nothing more perfect than bowl of rice, and nothing less appetizing than rice that is too wet or too dry.

COOKING PROCEDURE

Using the scoop, portion the rice into the cooking pot or rice cooker, never a precise measurement.

Then wash the rice, once or twice, adding cold water and swirling the rice around in it. This technique cleans the rice and releases some of the starch.

Drain the water, scrape the sides of the pot to loosen all the kernels stuck to the sides, and flatten the rice until it's even and level.

Then add more cold water. I never knew how much because we measured by finger. You put your index finger into the rice and used your thumb to mark how high the rice measured up to your finger. The water should double the mark.

You couldn't do it any other way or you risked a slap in the back of the head and a pretty good shaming. This is the only real way to cook rice.

Place the pot insert into the rice cooker, cover, and click the button. When the button clicks up, wait 10 minutes, and it will always come out perfect.

HOM DON YUK BANG (SALTED EGG MINCED PORK PIE)

This dish is an extremely popular dish in Chinese home cooking and has many different variations. It can be found on the Toisan table, Cantonese table, the Shanghainese table—we all love this dish. It's best steamed or panfried. Given its regional popularity, it can be compared to the American meat loaf, where almost every home has a different version sitting in its recipe box.

When I was kid, we would get hungry and very happy sitting at home, hearing the banging of the cleaver on the big wooden cutting board. It was a ten-minute constant rhythm of loud metal blows to wood, softened by chunks of perfect pork being chopped and prepared just to the right level of tenderness, where the texture after cooking holds in all the juiciness of the meat and yields just a touch of chewiness. Combined with water chestnuts, there is a particular snap on the first bite.

Traditionally, many love to top this dish with salted fish; others prefer mushrooms. The Toisanese, however, love their salted eggs.

1 PLATE, SERVES 6 | PREP TIME: 30 MINUTES | COOKING TIME: 30 MINUTES

INGREDIENTS

¾ pound pork belly, skin off

¼ pound pork butt

½ cup water chestnuts, peeled, washed, and small diced (fresh is preferred)

¼ cup thin soy sauce

3 tablespoons oyster sauce

½ tablespoon cornstarch

1½ egg whites, whipped to soft peaks

1 tablespoon vegetable oil

3 salted eggs*

1 tablespoon ginger, peeled and small diced

COOKING PROCEDURE

Hand chop the pork belly and pork butt, so it's finely minced. Mix the two meats together in a mixing bowl.

Next, incorporate the water chestnuts, the soy sauce, the oyster sauce, and the cornstarch, then fold in the egg whites.

Rub your hands with oil and mix all of the ingredients in the bowl, squeezing them together tightly until well combined. Place the meat mixture into a rimmed plate or very shallow bowl. Meanwhile, heat your Chinese steamer on high.

Separate the white and the yolks of the salted eggs, then cut the yolks in half and chop the whites. Put yolk halves and the chopped whites on the top of the pork and push into the meat slightly, then top with ginger.

Place in steamer for 30 minutes, or until done. You can stick a thermometer into the meat to make sure it's cooked through and 165°F.

Remove from the steamer and serve.

---

* Can be purchased fully cooked and prepared online or at most Chinese supermarkets.

STRING BEANS WITH FERMENTED TOFU

This is one of my favorite dishes of all time. The way the vegetables pair with the fermented tofu is sublime. Fermented tofu is an ingredient born from greatness. It has the texture of very soft cheese, so it acts like a paste that stands up to cooking with vegetables, which tend to release a lot of liquid. Tofu will meld with this liquid to make a pungent blast of savory deliciousness that coats your mouth. Add the sweetness of fresh and simply cooked vegetables properly balanced with some aromatics and you will create magic with this dish.

1 PLATE, SERVES 6 | PREP TIME: 20 MINUTES | COOKING TIME: 8 MINUTES

INGREDIENTS
1 tablespoon vegetable oil
¼ cup diced white onion
½ tablespoon minced ginger
¾ tablespoon minced garlic
½ pound string beans, haricots verts, or long beans; trimmed
½ cup chicken stock
1 tablespoon fermented tofu
1 tablespoon of the tofu liquid*
1 tablespoon thin soy sauce
1 tablespoon sliced scallions, for garnishing

COOKING PROCEDURE
In a pan or wok, add the vegetable oil on medium heat.

Add the onion, heat through for 2 minutes, then add the ginger and garlic, cooking the aromatics for 2 to 3 minutes or until soft.

Next, add the string beans and turn up the burner to high heat. Then add the chicken stock, the fermented tofu with its juice, and soy sauce. Allow to cook for 3 minutes.

Stir the curd until it blends into the stock and the mixture slightly thickens. Transfer to a platter and serve.

★ Fermented tofu can be purchased in the Chinese market or online. The jar will come with tofu sitting in a liquid that you can reserve.

BLUE CRABS DRY

After work, on occasion, my grandmother would come home with a large paper bag. She would set it on the table, then head into the other room to take her coat off and settle in from an afternoon of shopping. We wouldn't think anything was unusual until the bag started moving! We would hear something inside trying to get out and sometimes the bag would actually tip over. That meant we were eating crabs that night.

Back then, they weren't scarce or expensive, and they always seemed full of eggs, which isn't the case so much these days. Now, as they'd say on *The Honeymooners*, you need "a string of poloponies" to buy them. Regardless of how expensive they may be, Cantonese sautéed crabs "dry style" is still one of the best dishes you can eat.

1 PLATE, SERVES 6 | PREP TIME: 20 MINUTES | COOKING TIME: 12–15 MINUTES

INGREDIENTS

6 blue crabs, preferably live (see tip below)
¼ cup vegetable oil
1 tablespoon minced garlic
1 tablespoon minced ginger
¼ pound ground pork
½ cup water
½ tablespoon fermented black bean,* rinsed, dried, and crushed
2 tablespoons soy sauce
1 tablespoon oyster sauce
1 pinch white pepper
1 tablespoon MSG
2 eggs
1 scallion, sliced into rounds

COOKING PROCEDURE

Set wok or pan to medium heat and add the vegetable oil. Next, add the garlic and ginger, cook through for 2 minutes, and then increase the heat to high. Add the pork and let it sear until caramelized, about 2 to 3 minutes.

After the pork is cooked through and caramelized, add the crabs and top shells and shake. Pour in the water and let the mixture cook down until dry. (The water is not used to make a sauce; it is to ensure complete cooking of the crabs.)

Stir in the black bean, soy sauce, oyster sauce, white pepper, and MSG, then place a cover on your wok and continue cooking for 3 to 4 minutes. Remove cover and you will see the crab shells change color. Test for doneness by removing one piece and checking the color of the crabmeat. It should appear white when it's done. If it's still translucent, continue cooking, adding a little more water if needed.

Crack in the eggs and shake the pan or mix. As soon as the egg is cooked, about 1 minute, remove from the wok and place on a platter. Serve topped with scallions.

Tip:

Depending on the season, you should be able to see the crab eggs in the shell. Rinse off crabs, remove top shell with the eggs, and set aside. Remove gills and bottom tag, and discard. Cut the crab body in half. (This is traditionally done while the crab is still alive.) You can put a rubber band on the claws if you want to avoid the occasional pinch. If you prefer, you can blanch off the crabs first instead of cutting them in half while they are alive, then break them down.

---

*Can be purchased online or at most Chinese supermarkets.

STEAMED STRIPED BASS WITH BLACK BEANS

At most family gatherings, there will be a whole fish served. It's the centerpiece of dinner at the Chinese table. Everyone waits to plunge their chopsticks past the slightly clingy skin and into the sweet meat. You bring your catch back to your bowl of rice with an occasional slice of scallion and ginger, resting it there as you go back to spoon up some sauce to drizzle over the fish and let it seep into the rice below. Once this is accomplished, you can really start eating.

We always bring out the fish last at our table, which I believe is a form of parental control. Knowing that the fish will be devoured, parents temper their children's (and guest's) hunger a bit by letting them eat some of the other table offerings first to fill their stomachs before the main event. It's like the drumsticks at Thanksgiving dinner. No matter what, the family is gonna fight over them.

1 PLATE, SERVES 6 | PREP TIME: 10 MINUTES | COOKING TIME: 15–20 MINUTES

INGREDIENTS

2 small fingers ginger
2 scallions
¼ tablespoon fermented black beans*
1–1½ pounds striped bass (see tip below)
¼ cup soy sauce
¼ cup water
5 cilantro leaves
¼ cup vegetable oil
1 tablespoon sesame oil

Tip:

It is infinitely preferable if the bass is bought live out of the tanks at the Chinese market. Don't worry, they kill it for you there. Ask the fishmonger to clean, gut, and score it.

COOKING PROCEDURE

Peel and slice 1 finger of ginger into 2⅛-inch circle slices; julienne the other. Cut the green parts of the scallions into 1-inch segments and the white parts into thin slices. Wash your fermented black beans and pat them dry. Slightly crush them.

Begin by stuffing the cavity of the fish with the circle slices of ginger, half of the 1-inch green scallion segments, and a few fermented black beans.

Next, place the fish in a rimmed plate or shallow bowl wide enough to fit the fish. Pour the soy sauce on top of the fish and water into the bottom of the bowl. Place your steamer on high heat, and when it's at maximum steam, place the fish in the plate into the steamer.

Remove when the color of the fish's flesh is white and the temperature is approximately 135°F, about 15 minutes. (Don't spill the sauce. You'll regret it if you do.) Top the fish with the scallion whites and julienned ginger.

Add both oils to a saucepan on medium heat until you see one whiff of smoke. Remove from heat and pour the oil over the fish carefully, making sure to savor the sound of the sizzle. (Be careful: it may splatter!)

Garnish with cilantro, ginger julienne, and scallion whites, and serve with a pot of rice, six bowls, chopsticks, and love.

*Can be purchased online or at most Chinese supermarkets.

CHAPTER 4

CHASING THE PERFECT DUMPLING

I live in Brooklyn with my wife, Laura, and my son, Jeremy. A few years ago we were walking up the avenue and a few blocks away from our house was a little store with a "For Rent" sign. My wife said, "Why don't you see if you can rent it? Can't you imagine a little shop where you can make dumplings and snacks and cook really good Chinese food?" Two weeks later, we had a place with counters and little round stools. We called it East Wind Snack Shop.

"It's small, but we can make it into a place for everyone to love. We can hang a big TV on the wall and the kids can come enjoy good food and watch shows while their moms and dads can come and eat and relax. They can hang out up front and sit at the counter and have pork dumplings, spring rolls, and a bubble tea."

Decorated in red and white, we created not just a moment of inspiration, but a haven for it. I hope the kids who eat in my shop will grow up with the memories of savoring my dumplings and be inspired by them someday, just like the dumplings I ate as a kid in Chinatown inspired me.

The first few years after we opened East Wind, I was the only cook. So I really, *really*

focused on dumplings. I cooked each and every one myself, every single day. I worked the dough and folded up the dumplings fresh every morning. I was determined to cook every dumpling to order.

Through that rigorous daily regimen, I found myself wanting to know what made the best dumpling. That's the essence of working in a professional kitchen: You can only get it right by cooking the same thing over and over thousands of times. If you are a good cook, you will pay attention to every variable. Every mistake is an opportunity to learn. Of course, I learned a whole lot.

When you are analyzing and perfecting a dish, it's important to break it down to its base elements and look at them each intimately. Make the dough for the wrappers by hand fresh every day. Source the pork and combine the right cuts for the best fat content. Grind the meat yourself instead of buying it pre-ground.

As time went on, I examined the science and conditions necessary to cook them perfectly. How long should they set in the fridge before cooking? How much water should be added to the pan when cooking? Should I develop the crust of the dumpling before or after adding water to the pan? How long should I let them rest before eating?

I explored many variables that affect the art of dumpling making at East Wind, but what makes my dumplings so good at is that I stick to the discipline and traditions of the craft. Simple fundamentals—using high-quality meat, making them from scratch every day, and cooking to order—made them pretty close to perfect. Stick to that and all your dumpling dreams can come true, but the perfect dumpling only stays that way for a short time, like most perfect things.

The Elements of a Great Dumpling

There are four core components of dumplings: the wrapper, the filling, the cooking technique, and the accompanying sauce.

The Wrappers

This beginning phase of dumpling-making includes the folding. Folding is the thing that intimidates first-time dumpling makers the most. Let me be clear: This takes skill and practice. These techniques will take some time to learn and master, but figure it this way—you will have a blast trying to get it right and a lot of laughs on the first few attempts.

Each dumpling has a different fold. Some are really simple to make, while others take more practice to get them right. Take a picture of the dumplings you make the first time, then each subsequent batch. You will be proud of your progress. (Hell, Instagram it. Tag me, @chefchrischeung.)

The two most important ancient Chinese secrets for learning how to master folding are: 1) all the wrappers should be the same size and 2) use the same amount of filling for every dumpling. Consistency is everything. If you can do that, you're golden. Don't worry about the folding, you will get the hang of it. If you learned how to tie your shoelaces, you will be able to learn how to fold pretty dumplings.

You can buy packaged dumpling wrappers or you can make them from scratch. For some dumplings, it's just better to buy them; for others, to get great results, you need to make your own.

Wonton skins are better store-bought, as the machines that make them ensure their thinness is consistent, and the factory drying process makes it easier to steam or boil them without breakage. Soup dumplings, however, require making the dough and skin by hand (if you want good ones).

Store-Bought Wrappers	Making the Dough from Scratch
Easy to manage, no mess	The self-satisfaction of making it yourself
Consistent thinness/thickness	Control of thinness or thickness
Consistent pliability	The dough can be more pliable, softer, and bouncy
Energy/time saving, no dough to knead	Doesn't dry out as quickly, wrappers tend to last longer

Sealing the wrapper is different for each type. For store-bought machine-made wrappers, you will need to brush or use your finger to spread water or egg wash around the perimeter of the dumpling to seal.

Handmade dough you can just press without having to add what I like to call "dumpling glue." The water content in the dough is enough to seal the wrapper on its own. Make sure you fold and press directly around the filling. You need to squeeze out any air that could be trapped inside.

The Filling

If you go to Chinatown and order a dumpling, and you don't specify what type, most will have pork or shrimp, or a combination of the two.

You can grind or chop your own, or buy the meat pre-ground from the butcher. Just make sure it's a coarse grind, as this yields the best texture when eating a dumpling.

Many dumplings have some trace of seafood, whether freshly chopped or contained in the condiments (i.e. oyster sauce) that flavor the filling. Preserved seafood adds an extra intense savory flavor to Chinese food that makes it so damn good.

Soy sauce, scallions, ginger, garlic, and small minced vegetables like water chestnuts are also typical in most dumplings. Whatever you use, make sure you squeeze tightly when you mix your ingredients together. Get all the air out. It's a small detail, but one that can make the difference between good and great. This helps the liquids flow within the meat, making for a juicier dumpling.

Keep your filling cold until you are ready to assemble your dumplings. You will find it's way easier to scoop the same amount per dumpling and to fold into your wrapper. The dumplings retain their shape a whole lot better this way. Work in small batches and keep the rest of the filling in the refrigerator, re-upping as needed.

Storage

As you fold your dumplings, place them on a tray lined with parchment paper that has a touch of oil spread on it, so your dumplings won't stick. After you finish the tray, top with another sheet of parchment paper.

Refrigerate the assembled dumplings for about an hour before cooking. This lets the dough and filling set, and allows the dough to get a bit of its bounce back. It will also keep the fat of the pork filling cold, which, when cooked, will yield a more succulent dumpling.

Every dumpling has a life span. When you make the wrappers on your own, they will only last the day. The same is true for store-bought wrappers once opened. You can attempt to cook them the next day, but it's a lot like cooking gum. All the work you put into folding them will be gone. Prepare and cook them the day you want to eat them. If you really want to extend the life span of your dumplings, you can:

Freeze 'Em

There is a procedure for freezing dumplings. If you make your dumplings and put them in a container in the freezer, when you are ready to cook them, they will come out of that container as one massive dumpling glob.

Your next move of course will be to boil them from the glob stage. You will be able to salvage some of them as they cook, but you will also shake your head in shame over all the ones that are wasted.

To avoid this, place each one on a sheet pan with daylight between them in nice uniform rows. When the tray is full, place them in the freezer. Let them completely freeze. Once they are frozen, you can take them out of the freezer and place them in that same container or even a ziplock bag. Put them back in that freezer until you are hungry.

Please note: If you aren't that quick of a dumpling maker, the ones you have already made will start to get gummy and "melt" if you are cooking in a hot kitchen. Make ten and place the tray in the freezer, then make another ten when you're ready.

Parboil 'Em

You can also parboil the dumplings. Boil a large pot of water, as if you were cooking pasta, with about 3 gallons of water and ½ cup of vegetable oil.

Add your dumplings in batches. Scoop them out with a strainer and immerse them in ice water. Add some oil to the ice water as well. Leave them in the ice water for a minute to fully stop any carryover cooking. Strain and drain.

Put some in a bowl and coat with a tablespoon of oil, then line a container with parchment paper and place the dumplings in a single layer on the parchment paper. Wrap them up with some plastic wrap and reboil, steam, or sear them when hungry. (This is not a viable technique for soup dumplings, unfortunately.)

Cookery

Each style of dumpling has its own way of cooking. Potstickers are boiled and seared to finish. Shumai are steamed. Wontons can be boiled, served in soup, or even fried. These are classic cooking styles. You need to follow cooking times carefully since the meat is hidden within the wrapper, and it's tough to determine when it's done if you aren't focused. Make extra dumplings to taste test and to check doneness.

Sauces and Oils

Sauce is dictated by whoever is eating it. Some will drown their dumplings in soy and sriracha. Others use no sauce at all. Certain people can't eat them without vinegar. Check the market for condiments you may want to try, or use my Damn Good Dipping Sauce (see page 39) for anything you like, but it's best on dumplings.

If you like a spicy kick, there is nothing better than a good chili oil. Sichuan peppercorns aren't like karate boards; they like to hit back.

> Tip:
> Many dipping sauces do not require heat to make. Be aware, until the solid elements of the sauce like sugar fully dissolve, you cannot correctly judge the taste of the sauce.

SAUCES AND OILS

Damn Good Dipping Sauce

MAKE 3 CUPS | PREP TIME: 5 MINUTES | COOKING TIME: 3 MINUTES

INGREDIENTS

1 cup thin soy sauce
½ cup mushroom soy sauce
½ cup Chinkiang vinegar
¼ cup rice vinegar
½ cup sugar
1 tablespoon sesame oil
2 tablespoons chili paste
1 tablespoon MSG
1 dry chili, minced
¼ cup sliced scallions
1 tablespoon chopped cilantro

COOKING PROCEDURE

Add all of the ingredients in a bowl and mix until well incorporated.

Chili Oil

MAKES OVER A QUART OF CHILI OIL | PREP TIME: 10 MINUTES | COOKING TIME: 40 MINUTES (IN 2 STEPS)

INGREDIENTS

5 cups vegetable oil
½ cup sesame oil
4 cups whole dried chilies, slightly crushed
½ cup Sichuan peppercorns
4 cloves garlic, peeled and crushed
1 finger ginger, peeled and chopped
1 piece star anise
1 tablespoon kosher salt
½ tablespoon MSG

COOKING PROCEDURE

Mix the vegetable oil and sesame oil in saucepan on medium heat until you see one whiff of smoke.

While you are carefully watching the oil come up to temperature, mix the chilies, peppercorns, garlic, ginger, star anise, and salt in a large metal mixing bowl.

When the oil is ready, pour into the bowl, submerging all the chilies and aromatics. (Be careful. Make sure there is no water in the bowl or on the aromatics or the oil will splatter. Not kidding, this can be a dangerous step. You have to respect hot oil.)

Let it sit for 30 minutes and cool down. Add the MSG.

Strain out the aromatics the next day, or let it sit on the bottom to develop even more flavor with a little time.

TYPES OF DUMPLINGS

The dumplings highlighted in this chapter are a six-pack of the best-tasting, most popular, and most fun dumplings you can make. Included in this section are recipes, techniques, tips, and stories that celebrate the art of dumpling making.

SHUMAI

The shumai dumpling (also known as "sui mai" or "shaomai") is simple perfection. It's easy to make and is a top star on any dim sum menu. Like shrimp *har gow*, it's a treat to receive these from a dim sum cart and pull them off the bottom of the bamboo steamer. Tug them with your chopsticks and they will peel right off. Dip into some dumpling sauce and in two bites, they are gone!

The wrappers that make these dumplings are best bought at the market, but are available online as well. Buy the yellow round wonton wrappers. (Twin Marquis is a very popular brand.)

I like to think of these dumplings as the starter kit. There are different ways to wrap shumai, but as a beginner, your dumplings will look fine if you can form the skin around the meat since these are open-faced dumplings. Pleats are nice as you become more comfortable with folding, but these are great practice to just get a sense of how ground meat takes to the wrapper.

The filling is traditionally pork. I base most of my fillings on the salted egg minced pork pie my grandmother used to cook that I describe in the Sunday Dinner chapter. My mom and my aunts have mastered this Toisan classic, and they would scream, "ALWAYS HAND CHOP THE MEAT!" That's another ancient Chinese secret for dumpling filling. (I hope you consider buying a Chinese cleaver mentioned in the equipment section because hand-chopping your meat is one of those things that will separate you from the average dumpling maker.)

SHUMAI (CONTINUED)

MAKES AT LEAST 18 DUMPLINGS | PREP TIME: 25 MINUTES | COOKING TIME: 7 MINUTES

INGREDIENTS

½ pound pork, coarsely ground or hand-chopped

½ cup water chestnuts, minced

1 tablespoon minced ginger

1 teaspoon cornstarch

2 tablespoons oyster sauce

3 tablespoons thin soy sauce

½ egg white

1 pack thin yellow wonton circle wrappers

½ cup Damn Good Dipping Sauce (see page 39)

MAKING THE FILLING

Mix the pork, water chestnuts, ginger, cornstarch, oyster sauce, and thin soy sauce in a mixing bowl. Separately, whip a whole egg white to soft peaks, but only use half. When the pork mixture is well combined, fold in the egg white. Cover and refrigerate for 1 hour.

Tip:

This dumpling is cooked by simply steaming. Rub a little oil on the bottom of your cooking vessel so the shumai won't stick. Timing is a bit more important with these dumplings, as there will be minimal visual hints to let you know they are done. Firmness is a good indicator. Knowing there is a decent window of time before your dumplings start to overcook helps. Above all, to be sure, stick one with a meat thermometer to make sure it's 165°F.

ASSEMBLING THE DUMPLING

Place 1 tablespoon of filling in wonton circle. Next, place the wrapper in one hand and begin to mold around the filling. Pleat the wrapper with your dominant hand and secure the pleats as you turn the dumpling in your grip with your non-dominant hand.

When all folds are secured, keep rotating the dumpling in your grip while you mold filling in the dumpling wrapper. Tap the top with your dominant index finger and middle finger, and tap the bottom with your dominant thumb. This evens out the filling.

Place on paper-lined tray brushed with oil to store.

COOKING PROCEDURE

Space out the dumplings on an oiled level in steamer with daylight between them so the steamer is not overcrowded. Steam for approximately 7 minutes and check for doneness with a meat thermometer (165°F). Remove the dumplings from the steamer and place them on a serving platter.

Serve with Damn Good Dipping Sauce.

POTSTICKERS

According to legend, the emperor of China during some dynasty long ago ordered dumplings from his chef for lunch. In those days, dumplings were made only one way: boil and serve.

The chef followed all the traditional steps to make dumplings for His Highness. He hand-chopped the pork, sliced fresh scallions, added some water chestnuts, and mixed them all together so they were ready to be wrapped.

Then the chef mixed the flour with water and rolled out the dough, kneading it just right. After a short rest, he pinched a piece of that dough ball and pulled it off. With his rolling pin in hand, he formed a thin circle that he skillfully sealed around little scoops of filling so they were perfectly wrapped for the emperor. Like little soldiers all lined up, he marched them into the boiling water to cook.

"Aiya!" the chef said to himself, as he realized that he forgot to mix the dipping sauce and there was no more soy in his kitchen. He would have to go downstairs to finish his sauce where the new batch was kept. By the time he got back, all the water had boiled out of the pot, leaving the dumplings stuck to the bottom.

"WHERE ARE MY DUMPLINGS?!" the emperor started to scream.

Fearful for his life, the chef took a spatula and scraped the dumplings off the pan, and noticed a beautiful crispy bottom that made the dumpling look oddly tasty. Hoping for the best, he tossed them on the platter and off they went to the emperor. The chef luckily was not executed. In fact, the emperor loved them so much they became his favorite snack, and boom! The Legend of the Potsticker was born.

POTSTICKERS *(CONTINUED)*

MAKES AT LEAST 18 DUMPLINGS | PREP TIME: 25 MINUTES | COOKING TIME: 8 MINUTES

INGREDIENTS

For the Dough
1 pound all-purpose flour
1 tablespoon salt
7 ounces simmering water

For the Filling
½ pound pork, coarsely ground and hand-chopped
½ tablespoon fermented black beans,* crushed into a paste
2 tablespoons oyster sauce
½ tablespoon minced garlic
½ tablespoon minced ginger
3 tablespoons soy sauce
2 tablespoons scallions, sliced
3 tablespoons water chestnuts, minced

For the Cooking
½ tablespoon vegetable oil
12 dumplings
1 cup water
½ cup Damn Good Dipping Sauce (see page 39)

MAKING THE DOUGH

Prepare your mixer with hook attachment and set to the slowest speed.

Add the flour and salt to the mixer bowl then add in half of the hot water. Mix, gradually adding more water so all the flour from the bottom of the bowl is incorporated. Every environment is different, so you may need a little more water or a little less to get the correct results.

Mix until it forms a ball of dough that is slightly sticky, soft, and pliable. Leave the mixture in the bowl to mix for an additional 10 minutes.

Take the dough out of bowl, knead it slightly, wrap it with plastic wrap, and refrigerate overnight.

MAKING THE FILLING

Place all filling ingredients in a mixing bowl and mix until incorporated. Squeeze the mixture tightly to eliminate any air pockets. Refrigerate for 1 hour.

> Tip:
> Potstickers, ironically, are best cooked in nonstick pans. Once these beauties hit the pan, it's all about temperature control. This ensures a proper cook and brilliant sear.

---

* Can be purchased online or at most Chinese supermarkets.

MAKING THE WRAPPERS

Cut the dough in quarters. On your work surface, work each piece of dough into a log 1 foot long by ½ inch wide without any dusting flour.

With a bench cutter, cut the logs into nuggets the size of the tip of your pinky, weighing half an ounce. Dust with flour, and loosely cover all with a sheet of plastic wrap to prevent drying. (At the start, intend on making one dumpling at a time. As you get faster, you can roll out 10 wrappers at a time.)

Dust work surface with flour, then take a nugget and roll into a ball between the palms of your hands. Place the ball on your work surface and dust it with flour.

Flatten the ball with heel of your palm, then take your rolling pin and dust it. Roll and flatten the perimeter of the circle. You will not roll the inner ½-inch radius of the skin; just roll back and forth along the perimeter so the edges are thinner.

Dust as needed to prevent sticking to your worktable. The thinness and size of the wrapper from this point is up to you and the particular dumpling. For potstickers, medium thickness, about ⅟₁₆-inch thick (too thin of a skin may break when cooking), is appropriate. The diameter of the wrapper should turn out to be about a total of approximately 2 inches. You can roll out slightly larger for easier folding.

You now have a circle wrapper ready to be folded into a dumpling. I am right-handed, so these next steps are designed for right-handed people. Reverse for left-handed folding. Please note: I'm sure there are some small differences in the feel for folding if you are left-handed.

FOLDING THE DUMPLINGS

No matter which fold, for a 2-inch circle, you should use approximately 1 tablespoon of filling. (You may have to adjust to an amount that you feel comfortable folding with.) At first, a little less, and then with practice, you can push it a bit more to give you luscious fatty pillows of deliciousness.

The Pretty Front-Pleated Dumpling (pictured on page 50)

Place your wrapper in your hand and scoop the filling into the middle of your dumpling wrapper. Fold one side over the other, so it looks similar to a taco shell or a half-moon, but do not seal. For store-bought wrappers, you will need to moisten the perimeter with water to seal them. For fresh dough wrappers, this is not necessary.

Pinch the far-left side with your left thumb and index finger. Hold this grip while cradling the bottom of the dumpling on your left middle, ring, and pinky fingers. Your left thumb and index finger should stay in this position through the whole fold, but left your thumb slightly lifts up to lightly press the pleats made by your right thumb.

Both of your hands should work in synchronization to create the pleats. With your right thumb, push the front edge of the wrapper to the left, making the first pleat. Continue by pushing the pleat left, letting your left thumb "collect the pleat" and then using your right thumb to make another pleat. About six to eight pleats will do, until you reach the far right side of the dumpling.

Next, press along the top edge of the dumpling to seal the pleats to the back flap. At the top right of the dumpling, where you made the last pleat, fold the last corner back.

Finally, shape the dumpling by gently pulling up on the sealed part and down on the fat part. This will also squeeze out any excess air.

No-Pleat Easy-Fold Dumpling

This general fold is used for potstickers, among many other dumplings, including *sui gow*.

Place your filling in the middle of the wrapper, and fold in half over the filling, sealing to close. Push down until you feel the filling and push out any excess air pockets. Place on a sheet pan pushing down a bit to flatten at the bottom.

COOKING PROCEDURE

Heat an 11-inch nonstick pan to medium heat and add the vegetable oil. Place your dumplings in the pan. Don't overcrowd!

Add your water about half way up on the dumplings and cover your pan. Turn up the heat to maximum. Cook for approximately 4 to 8 minutes. Note: Cooking times vary, depending on the size of the pan, type of stove, etc. Turn the heat down back to medium as you see the water reducing and the pan is almost dry. You will see big bubbles in the pan.

Lift cover and let the dumplings sear on the dry pan to form the crust on the bottom of the dumplings, about 2 minutes or until golden brown.

Transfer dumplings to a platter and serve with Damn Good Dipping Sauce, chili oil, or both.

SOUP DUMPLINGS

The most well-kept secret to soup dumplings isn't how to make the wrapper thin or how to get the soup into the dumpling—it's how to eat them. I've seen plenty of rookies bite right in, burn their mouth, and splatter the soup all over the table. It's Shanghai's revenge, death by soup burn and humiliation.

Here is how to eat it properly: Place your dumpling on a Chinese spoon, bite off the little spout on the top, and spoon in a little Chinkiang vinegar, which will temper the hot soup inside. Then slurp it all up, and finish by popping the rest of the dumpling in your mouth. International incident avoided.

Many fans of these dumplings rate them on the thinness of the wrapper. It certainly is an art form to develop enough gluten in a paper-thin skin that holds the bubbling soup inside the dumpling as you cook it. Off the mainland of China, they have adopted this highly skilled method to make these bad boys, but it has to be noted that these were originally invented on the mainland in Shanghai, where they appreciate a thicker skin and, thus, a heartier dumpling.

Since it's mostly liquid, the extra chew from the skin makes for a more filling meal. You be the judge, delicate or hearty. You can buy white dumpling wrappers for medium thickness or wonton skins for a thin, delicate soup dumpling. Make your own dough if you want to control the thickness of the wrapper yourself.

If this is your first introduction to this great snack, please try them at the restaurant first. It's a very complicated dumpling that makes so much delicious sense after eating a few made by a professional. It will also give you the motivation to match their skill and experience the glory of conquering the steps needed to make these dumplings at home.

> **Tip:**
> You do not have to make broth yourself with pork bones. You can purchase pork broth or pork base (or even chicken base) in bouillon cubes. Skip the bones to make the broth and follow the directions to make it into a jelly. Adjust the flavor and salt content to taste.

SOUP DUMPLINGS (CONTINUED)

MAKES AT LEAST 18 DUMPLINGS | PREP TIME: 3½ HOURS, REST OVERNIGHT
COOKING TIME: 8–10 MINUTES

INGREDIENTS

For the Dough
1 pound all-purpose flour
1 tablespoon salt
7 ounces simmering water

For the Broth Filling
5 pounds pork bones (or
    1–2 pork or chicken bouillon
    cubes per gallon)
1 white onion, quartered
1 finger ginger, peeled
1 gallon water or to just cover
    bones in pot
2 cups oyster sauce
1 cup soy sauce
½ cup Shaoxing wine*
10 pieces dried mushroom
2 pieces star anise
2 tablespoons MSG
    (use sparingly if using
    bouillon cubes)
2 cups cold water
2 cups gelatin

MAKING THE DOUGH

Set your mixer with hook attachment on lowest setting. Pour your flour and salt in mixer bowl, and then half of the water.

Mix, gradually adding more water until all the flour from the bottom of bowl is incorporated. Mix until the ball of dough is slightly sticky, soft, and pliable. Rest in the bowl to mix for an additional 10 minutes. Every environment is different, so the amount of water you need to get the correct results may vary.

Take the dough out of the bowl and knead slightly, then wrap with plastic wrap and rest in your refrigerator overnight.

Cut the dough in quarters. On your work surface, work dough into a log 1 foot long by ½ inch wide on your work surface without any dusting flour.

With a bench cutter, cut into nuggets the size of your pinky tip, weighing 0.5 ounce. Dust with flour and loosely cover all the dough nuggets with a sheet of plastic wrap to prevent drying. (At the start, intend on making one dumpling at a time. As you get faster, you can roll out 10 wrappers at a time.)

Take a nugget and roll it into a ball between the palms of your hands. Dust your work surface with flour and place the ball of dough on the surface, then dust the ball of dough with flour.

Flatten the ball with heel of your palm. Take your rolling pin and dust it, then roll and flatten the perimeter of the circle. Do not roll the inner ½-inch radius of the wrapper; just roll back and forth along the perimeter and stay away from the middle.

Dust as needed to prevent the wrappers from sticking to worktable. If you want a thin wrapper, your circle should be the same size as potsticker wrappers, maybe a touch larger, roughly 2½ inches in diameter. You can make your wrappers thicker starting with a

---

* Can be purchased online or at most Chinese supermarkets.

For the Pork and Crab Filling

1½ pound gelatinized pork broth

½ pound crabmeat (buy fresh-picked blue crab or frozen)

½ pound ground pork, coarse grind/hand-chopped

3 tablespoons oyster sauce

1 tablespoon minced garlic

1 tablespoon minced ginger

¼ cup soy sauce

4 tablespoons sliced scallions

For the Cooking

½ napa cabbage, sliced thin

1 cup Chinkiang vinegar

0.7-ounce nugget of dough. The latter is preferable for beginners to avoid breakage.

Even in the case where you make thinner wrappers for soup dumplings, the wrappers should really only be thin on the sides. The bottom should be left a bit thicker to prevent tearing and the tops get thicker as you fold the pleats onto each other.

MAKING THE BROTH FILLING

There is a lot of nuance in this filling. You need to first make a broth, either using pork bones or a pork bouillon cube, then you will need to make the broth into a jelly with gelatin powder.

Roast the pork bones until browned, about 5 minutes. Place the bones in a pot with onion and ginger. Cover with water, then add the oyster sauce, soy sauce, Shaoxing wine, mushrooms, and star anise. Simmer for 2 hours.

If you're making the broth using the bouillon cubes, follow the instructions on the box, then complete the instructions below.

Add the MSG, then remove from the heat and strain. Add the cold water to the gelatin powder and let it bloom, about 3 to 5 minutes. Add 2 cups of bloomed gelatin to 1 quart of simmered pork broth. Stir well to fully incorporated.

Refrigerate overnight and the next day you should have a tight jelly. Small dice.

In a separate bowl, mix the crab, pork, oyster sauce, garlic, ginger, soy sauce, and scallions well.

Take 2 cups of the pork and crab mixture and combine with 3½ cups of the jelly, squeezing well to incorporate. Please note: the proper ratio is important.

Cover and refrigerate for 1 hour.

ASSEMBLING THE DUMPLINGS (PICTURED ON PAGE 57)

There is one general style that is recognized for soup dumplings, although there are slightly different variants of this fold, depending on the folder and region.

Holding the wrapper in your non-dominant hand, place one tablespoon of filling in the middle of the wrapper. Pinch the skin with your thumb and index finger of your dominant hand and begin to create a small pleat. Secure the pleat with your dominant thumb and index finger.

Continuing to cradle the dumpling in your non-dominant hand, use your non-dominant thumb and index fingers to fold back each subsequent pleat toward you.

Extend your dominant index finger to collect each pleat as you work circularly around the perimeter. On the last pleat, twist slightly up and connect the edges to seal.

Make sure that you don't pack this filling into the wrapper and squeeze the air out like the other dumplings. The contents should feel slightly loose inside. The gelatin will melt into the soup and simmer inside the dumpling, so it needs room to breathe and expand. Since the broth separates from the meat and bubbles up to the top, the amount of filling you put into each wrapper matters.

COOKING PROCEDURE

Set your steamer to high, then layer the top level of the steamer with the napa cabbage (sometimes the water will boil over into the first level). Place the dumplings on top of the cabbage with daylight between them and cover tightly.

Steam for 6 to 7 minutes. (You can use an instant-read thermometer to check to see if the internal temperature is 165°F, but be prepared to lose a dumpling in the process.)

Remove the steamer basket from the base and serve the soup dumplings in the basket with Chinkiang vinegar and Chinese spoons. Slurp and enjoy.

SUI GOW (WATER DUMPLINGS)

This may be the one dumpling to rule them all. I think most iterations of dumplings are derived from these. You can interchange skins, fillings, and cooking methods as you like. The only characteristics necessary are to make them big and hearty!

Sui gow dumplings (also known as "*soy gow,*" "*sui kow,*" and "*shui jiao*") are made at home frequently during celebrations. There is nothing like a whole family busting out dozens of dumplings, everyone looking around the room and judging each other's dumpling-making abilities. When I was a kid, all the family's best dumpling makers would stand around the kitchen table, and my mom would put out the bowl of filling stabbed with a spoon for each of us (and the rare wooden dumpling paddle or even butter knife, when the spoons ran out).

My cousins and I weren't cooks (yet), so we opened the packages of dumpling wrappers and filled the little bowls of water for sealing. Blowing flour at your cousin was always part of the fun. Our dumplings were never the same size, we always made a mess, and there would be an occasional fight. It was beautiful chaos. Overall, it was a great time, especially when we got to eat. The dumplings somehow still always looked perfect after my mom served them, and I always thought that was strange.

MAKES AT LEAST 18 DUMPLINGS | PREP TIME: 30 MINUTES | COOKING TIME: 5 MINUTES

INGREDIENTS
½ pound pork, coarsely ground or hand-chopped
½ pound 16/20 shrimp, peeled, deveined, coarsely chopped
½ tablespoon fermented black beans,* crushed into a paste
3 tablespoons oyster sauce
1½ tablespoon minced garlic
1½ tablespoon minced ginger
¼ cup soy sauce
4 tablespoons scallions, sliced
½ cup water chestnuts, minced
1 pack white dumpling wrappers
1 cup water
¼ cup vegetable oil
1 cup Damn Good Dipping Sauce (see page 39)

MAKING THE FILLING
Place pork, shrimp, fermented black beans, oyster sauce, garlic, ginger, soy sauce, scallions, and water chestnuts in a mixing bowl and mix until incorporated. Squeeze tightly to eliminate any air pockets. Cover and refrigerate for 1 hour.

ASSEMBLING THE DUMPLINGS
With your finger, rub water around the perimeter of the dumpling skin. Place 1¼ tablespoons filling in the skin and fold up. Gently squeeze out any air and seal. Place the finished dumplings on your sheet pan and press down a bit.

COOKING PROCEDURE
Set your pot of blanching water to boil and add the vegetable oil. Drop the dumplings in, but don't overcrowd the pot.

Cook the dumplings for approximately 4 minutes. Check for doneness, 165°F with your thermometer.

Strain out with a spider to a platter and serve with Damn Good Dipping Sauce.

★ Can be purchased online or at most Chinese supermarkets.

Tip:

This dumpling is all about the shrimp and a touch of bamboo shoots. Hand chop for dumplings that pop! That will get you that traditional texture. Bamboo shoots may be available fresh in the Chinese market, but if not available, you can use the canned version. Drop a hint of cornstarch, salt, MSG, and those shoots, and you are ready to get cookin'.

HAR GOW
(CRYSTAL SHRIMP DUMPLINGS)

Har gow (or *Xia Jiao*) shrimp dumplings are a classic dim sum specialty and have become a signature dish at my shop. I've eaten these all my life. My Uncle Sai, who owned a Chinatown coffeehouse when I was little, taught me how to make these the traditional way.

A mix of wheat starch, tapioca starch, and potato starch makes the skin. If you are a dumpling-making rookie, but insist on making everything from scratch, you may want to start with a flour-based dumpling as this dough is a little harder to manage. These are unlike any dumplings you have made before, and making them properly is far from simple.

Har gow dumplings are classically steamed. They become semitranslucent as they cook. The shrimp filling will plump up and the orange tint will appear as if it's about to burst through the silky bubble of dough.

They are naturally gluten-free, as the filling has no soy sauce and the wrappers are made with wheat starch (which has been separated from the protein that would develop gluten). Please note: You can't buy these wrappers; you have to make them by hand.

If you want to make the wrappers the traditional way, you also need a special cleaver that is made without a cutting edge, which you will slap the side of onto a dough ball and press it until it creates a circle. This is what keeps them uniform and consistent. That is the old-school way. (Some advice, since this technique is not easy to teach through written instructions and you may not have a cleaver: Use your rolling pin and you'll be fine.)

Despite following all of the old-school traditions of making *har gow*, I throw an even more diabolical layer of kitchen creativity onto this dumpling. I wanted to push the envelope, and felt it needed a crunchy element. Therefore, I developed a tapioca crust, which made the skin crispy, chewy, crunchy, and silky all at the same time. I offer my contribution to the evolution of this dish knowing the Chinese food community is watching me closely. This new style of *har gow* calls for steaming in the pan and then searing to finish, so the dumplings should slide right onto the plate, riding their crusts. The steaming is still there to activate the translucent effect on the skin and will keep the shrimp juicy and tasty.

Many strict traditionalists (especially in my own family) have remarked on their uncertainty if this new style was going to be acceptable. However, the unique mouthfeel of the classic skin and the hand-chopped shrimp is amplified by a crispy, sticky tapioca crust that has turned even the most skeptical into very happy eaters. I give you the "tricked-out *har gow*." May it live forever.

HAR GOW (CONTINUED)

MAKES 16 DUMPLINGS | PREP TIME: 40 MINUTES | COOKING TIME: 8 MINUTES

INGREDIENTS

For the Wrappers
4 ounces wheat starch
¾ ounce tapioca starch
¾ ounce potato starch
1 cup boiling water
1 ounce vegetable oil

For the Filling
½ pound 16/20 shrimp,
    peeled, deveined, and
    coarsely chopped
⅛ cup minced bamboo shoots,*
½ tablespoon salt
1 tablespoon MSG

Tapioca Batter
¾ cup tapioca starch
1 cup cold water

Cooking Ingredients
½ tablespoon vegetable oil
    (plus ½ tablespoon for each
    round of dumplings)
4 dumplings
3 tablespoons tapioca batter
1 cup water
½ cup abalone sauce
    (preferably Lee Kum Kee)

COOKING PROCEDURE

Making the Dough
Prepare your mixer with paddle attachment and place on setting 2. Place the wheat starch, tapioca starch, and potato starch in mixer bowl.

Add the water slowly and mix until it's smooth and pliable. Add oil and knead well. Wrap in plastic wrap and rest for 30 minutes.

Making the Filling and Tapioca Batter
Mix shrimp with bamboo shoots, salt, and MSG. Cover and refrigerate for 1 hour.

Add the cold water to the starch and stir well until it has dissolved.

Assembling Dumplings
Cut the ball of dough in half. Roll one half of the dough into a long log, approximately 1 foot long by ½ inch wide. Cut ¾-inch nuggets off the log. Press a nugget down with palm of your hand. Use a rolling pin to flatten into a thin circle.

Place a ½ tablespoon of filling into the circle and fold over. With practice, you can incorporate pleats into the fold. See instructions for pleated folding on pages 50–51.

Cooking the Dumplings
Heat an 11-inch nonstick pan on medium heat and ½ tablespoon vegetable oil. Add 4 dumplings close together in pan, then spoon 3 tablespoons of tapioca batter into the bottom of the pan.

Next, add 1 cup of water to pan, cover, and turn to high heat. When the water has almost evaporated from pan, remove the lid, and let the bottom crust crisp up.

Slide the whole crust onto a plate and serve. Repeat process as many times as needed.

Spoon a tablespoon of abalone sauce on each portion.

---

* Can be purchased online or at most Chinese supermarkets.

WONTON NOODLE SOUP

There are times when you have to accept hard truths that life throws right in your face. You can't make a good wonton soup without MSG. It is a necessary flavor that—when combined with plump fat dumplings, pork broth, some scallions, and white pepper—magically transports you to a magnificent noodle dream, where you're holding a weird big white spoon and slurping up silky clouds of goodness. Reconfigure your brain waves through each spoon of broth with a savoriness that coats your tongue and takes you to a happy place that only a few dishes in this world can do. That's a good wonton noodle soup.

There is something comforting about a hot bowl of Cantonese wonton noodle soup that makes everyone warm and fuzzy. This truly great dish has transcended time. It has gone from a humble Chinese classic to an iconic Chinese American bowl of awesome.

MAKES 6 BOWLS | PREP TIME: 3½ HOURS | COOKING TIME: 10 MINUTES

INGREDIENTS

For the Broth
2 pounds pork bones (or 2 pork bouillon)
1 pound fish bones (or 1 shrimp bouillon)
1 cup shrimp shells
1 gallon water
2 pieces star anise
1 cup Shaoxing wine*
¼ cup soy
2 tablespoons Chinese sugar
3 tablespoons MSG
1 tablespoon white pepper

For the Filling
¼ pound shrimp, peeled, deveined, and
    coarsely chopped
½ pound pork, coarsely ground
2 tablespoons oyster sauce
3 tablespoons soy sauce

1 tablespoon MSG
1 tablespoon kosher salt
1 teaspoon pepper
½ cup sliced scallion
1 tablespoon peeled and minced ginger
½ cup minced water chestnuts

For the Wontons
1 cup water
24 wonton wrappers

Finishing Touches
2 pounds thin wonton noodles*
12 bok choy leaves
6 scallions, sliced
6 cilantro leaves, chopped

---

* Can be purchased online or at most Chinese supermarkets.

COOKING PROCEDURE

For the Broth

Combine all broth ingredients in a stockpot and simmer for 3 hours. Skim the fat off the top of the broth and then strain the broth.

Making the Filling

Place the shrimp, pork, oyster sauce, soy sauce, MSG, salt, pepper, scallion, ginger, and water chestnuts in a large bowl and mix until incorporated. Cover and refrigerate for 1 hour.

Assembling the Dumplings

Rub water around the perimeter of the wonton wrapper. Place ¾ tablespoon of the filling in the center of the wrapper, fold up, squeeze air out, and seal. Transfer your wontons to a parchment-paper-lined sheet pan brushed with oil, cover with plastic wrap, and refrigerate for 1 hour.

Cooking

Heat your blanching water to a boil. In separate pot, heat your broth in a pot to a simmer.

Place 12 wontons in the blanching water for 3 to 4 minutes and transfer to bowls; repeat for 12 remaining wontons. If the noodles are fresh, cook for 2 to 3 minutes. For dry noodles, follow the instructions on the package. Transfer to bowls.

Add bok choy to the blanching water for 1 minute and transfer to bowls. Ladle the broth into the bowls.

Garnish with scallions and cilantro. Get warm and fuzzy with 5 friends.

CHAPTER 5

CHINESE AMERICAN CUISINE

I'm one of the few lucky ones to have had the experience of sitting down to eat and talk food with the late, great Anthony Bourdain.

On his show *No Reservations*, I had the pleasure of being his guide to the three Chinatowns of New York City. We explored the food malls of Flushing and ate hand-pulled noodles. We sat through the craziness of weekend morning dim sum in Sunset Park, Brooklyn. Yet the meal he was most excited for was in Manhattan's Chinatown, where we ate Chinese food classics he had eaten as a child. Growing up in New Jersey, his Sunday dinners at the neighborhood Chinese restaurant were filled with roast pork fried rice, sweet-and-sour shrimp, General Tso's chicken, and beef and broccoli.

Of course, eating with him, naturally, you get to talking. He had a way of peeling off layers in conversation to reveal a story or curiosity he wanted from you that was coaxed out through food. That was his superpower. The conversation always started with the food, and then, after a few shots of cognac, there would be an underlying discussion on culture, politics, or some other raw topic that the whole world would relish listening to.

Our time together centered on Chinatown restaurant phantom menus—how his family would eat General Tso's chicken and spare ribs as mine would eat from another menu altogether, with black bean snails, snow pea shoots with fermented tofu, and panfried flounder. In his eyes, the thing that really made that image something special was that our families could eat those meals next to each other, and both would be having the same great time.

The fact these things could coexist in the same restaurant describes the best of what America is, and seemed to take him to a place where he was truly happy. It reinforced his opinion that good food brings people together, and he certainly appreciated that Chinese restaurants went to the extra effort to cook food that he really liked as a kid.

This was special, because it happened in America, let alone in his hometown. He was now a part of an important piece of American culture, the Chinese restaurant. We made his childhood a happy one while securing our American dream.

The author and Anthony Bourdain enjoying a meal at Hop Kee, one of the oldest restaurants in Manhattan's Chinatown.

The Chinese American Restaurant

The lineage of Chinese American food starts in the countryside home cooking of Toisan. This food inspired the restaurant chefs of greater Guangdong. Those chefs were enticed (or maybe even forced) to go to Hong Kong for economic reasons, and made history with their level of cooking there. They developed many classic seafood dishes and expanded the use of expensive ingredients like abalone and shark fin. They also created the modern dim sum menu that is enjoyed worldwide today.

A lot of those chefs eventually migrated to America. Whether they were big-time chefs and had contracts to premier expensive midtown joints, or poor immigrants who just knew how to kick ass in the kitchen and made their living by working hard in Chinatown, they all spread the beauty of Chinese cuisine in America.

This migration ignited a Chinese-food phenomenon in America, a restaurant boom that I witnessed firsthand growing up. A Chinese restaurant became different things depending on its location.

The suburban establishments—found in Long Island, New Jersey, and other relaxed and well-to-do areas outside of New York City—captured the essence of Chinatown restaurants, as many of the chefs and owners got their start in the city. They were big places serving dumplings, spare ribs, pu pu platters, and noodles alongside General Tso's chicken, kung pao shrimp, and egg foo yong. Whole communities gathered there, especially on the weekend. These restaurants created a dining experience that is now embedded in the memories of the generations of countless American families.

Then there were the small neighborhood spots in the five boroughs, the take-out joints. The cooking in these kitchens had to be really cheap and fast, and fueled their communities for everyday lunches and dinners with fried chicken wings, egg rolls, and fried rice.

In midtown, there were also big banquet palaces that brought in star chefs from China, offered expensive wine, specialized in big parties, and stayed on the edge of contemporary Chinese cooking.

Then, of course, there is Chinatown. Teahouses, dim sum places, BBQ joints, noodle counters, and restaurants that catered to tourists as well as Chinese locals at the same time.

All are Chinese American restaurants.

The dishes in this chapter will bring you back to a simpler time, where you and the family were in the old station wagon headed to dinner at the neighborhood Chinese restaurant in the suburbs or taking a trip into Chinatown. Take a table next to my family's and Bourdain's. Recreate that nostalgia here with some of my favorite dishes.

Note:

From this point on, many of the recipes in the following chapters have basic techniques that are used in Chinese restaurant kitchens. Here are the recipes, techniques, and procedures that you will see reoccurring throughout the book.

BASIC TECHNIQUES FOR COOKING

Slurry

A cornstarch slurry is a big part of Chinese cuisine. It thickens our sauces, in place of things like xantham gum and roux. It's easy to make and takes a second to learn how to use. It is a bit misunderstood, and is one of the criticisms of Chinese cooking in America. People say the sauces are gloppy to the point that if it contains cornstarch they believe it couldn't possibly be good.

All I will say is that if you mix cornstarch with water into a loose paste, bring your sauce to its first bubble before it boils, add the slurry, mix until well combined, then bring it back to a boil and immediately stop any further cooking, your sauce will be perfectly thickened with no "gloppiness." You can adjust it as needed. Make sure you focus through the whole process, as some sauces like to boil over the second you look to something else.

YIELDS 1 CUP

INGREDIENTS
½ cup cornstarch
½ cup cold water

COOKING PROCEDURE
Pour cornstarch into the water and mix well. (If not immediately used, stir frequently until it's used.)

To thicken a sauce, add approximately ¼ cup of slurry per quart of bubbling sauce and stir well. Once it comes back to a boil, evaluate the thickness of the sauce. The amount of slurry varies with each recipe.

Velveting

Many meats that are stir-fried will go through an additional process in the Chinese kitchen called "velveting." This technique breaks down the tough fibers in meat, yielding a specific texture while preserving the protein. It's a common technique in Cantonese cooking and it's used to tenderize beef, pork, and poultry. A mixture of cornstarch, egg, wine, and baking soda is used as a marinade. The marinade and a little time will break down some of the connective tissue in the meat and simultaneously preserve it. When it's cooked, it yields a soft and velvety texture that is distinctive to the technique.

YIELDS APPROX. 1 CUP

INGREDIENTS
4 ounces cornstarch
2 eggs
2 tablespoons Shaoxing wine*
1 teaspoon baking soda

COOKING PROCEDURE
Place all ingredients in a mixing bowl and mix with a whisk until it's smooth. Marinating and cooking times vary based on the recipe. Be sure to cover and refrigerate while marinating.

Mushroom Water

It's a simple, savory, and intense liquid that I have developed to enhance many recipes in a way that Western cultures use highly concentrated stocks that are reduced for hours on their stovetops. You get a deep, savory flavor without all that time and energy. Not to mention, it's fully vegan. Many don't like mushrooms, but they will not be able to discern them as a single isolated flavor when cooking with mushroom water. Mushroom water takes all the flavors that are condensed in a mushroom's dried form (thanks to the science of Chinese cuisine) and intensifies it in water. I use this to increase flavor and replace or add to recipes that call just for stock or water alone. Just a heads-up: it's not a traditional ingredient; it's something that I have personally contributed to these recipes. You can use any dried mushroom as long as it suits your expectation of flavor. I use dried medium shiitakes, which are usually found in packaged bags at the Chinese markets, but you can find these easily online as well.

YIELDS 1 QUART

INGREDIENTS
2 cups dried mushrooms*
   (medium-sized shiitake)
1 quart of cold water

COOKING PROCEDURE
Place the dried mushrooms in a large container and pour the water over the mushrooms. Cover the container in plastic wrap or top with a lid. Let the mixture rest overnight in your refrigerator.

Strain out the liquid and reuse the dried mushrooms as a component in the recipe or save for another recipe.

---

* Can be purchased online or at most Chinese supermarkets.

Flash-Frying

This technique is used frequently in the Cantonese kitchen. When something is flash-fried, that means that you submerge meat, seafood, or vegetables in very hot oil, and then toss it into the wok to finish cooking. It's like par-frying, but much quicker. The technique imparts flavor through the oil, draws out the moisture from whatever you are cooking, and cuts the length of the cooking time. It is commonly used with velveted meats as part of the process that changes the texture of the protein. Many Cantonese kitchens have a wok sitting on high, filled with oil on standby, just for this technique.

INGREDIENTS/EQUIPMENT
1 deep pot or stockpot
Vegetable oil filling ⅔ of the pot
Dry spider or strainer

COOKING PROCEDURE
You will need a pot filled with oil at 350°F and large enough to dunk your spider or strainer into it comfortably. That temperature is high because you will not be frying for an extended time, depending on the size of what you are frying.

Note: Be careful! Don't bring water anywhere near this, and watch for any wet utensils like your spider that may have been used for blanching water. If it gets into the oil, it will splatter everywhere and potentially burn you. Keeps these utensils dry. You can cool the oil down after cooking, strain, and reuse for the next recipe.

Note on Blanching:

In the kitchen, you should also have a pot of water on for quick-blanching ingredients. Blanching is the close cousin of flash-frying, only you use water instead of oil. Vegetables and noodles are primarily what you will use this technique for. Keep this water clean and at a rolling boil. You will need to dunk like layups never existed every now and then.

EGG DROP SOUP

This simple soup is enriched with the ribbons of eggs streamed into soothing bone broth. It all comes together in the last step, where you swirl the pot or wok as the eggs hit the broth. It's like patting your head and rubbing your stomach at the same time, but with eggs.

MAKES 6 BOWLS OF SOUP | PREP TIME: 10 MINUTES | COOKING TIME: 6 MINUTES

INGREDIENTS

1 cup chicken thigh meat, skin removed, small diced

2 quarts chicken stock

½ cup Shaoxing wine*

¼ cup soy sauce

1 tablespoon chili-garlic paste (Sambal Olek is a good brand)

1 teaspoon white pepper

1 tablespoon MSG

¼ cup slurry (see page 69)

2 eggs, beaten

3 tablespoons sliced scallion

3 tablespoons minced cilantro

COOKING PROCEDURE

Blanch your diced chicken thighs for 2 minutes. Separately, bring the chicken stock to a simmer in your wok or saucepan, then add in the chicken thighs.

Next, add the Shaoxing wine, soy sauce, chili-garlic paste, white pepper, and MSG. Simmer for 4 minutes to ensure chicken is fully cooked. Bring up to a boil, add the slurry, and stir.

Turn the heat to very low. Using a ladle or a wok spoon, hold the beaten eggs over the broth and swirl the pan or wok carefully as you gradually pour the egg into the revolving broth. You will see the ribbons of egg slightly cooking in the broth.

Once all of the egg is incorporated, transfer to six soup bowls, garnish with scallion and cilantro, and serve with a Chinese soup spoon immediately as the egg can overcook in the hot broth.

---

* Can be purchased online or at most Chinese supermarkets.

GENERAL TSO'S CHICKEN

Whoever invented this dish definitely deserves to be in the cooking hall of fame. Legend has it that it either inspired Chicken McNuggets or McDonald's took the dish as their own after trying to buy the recipe for a few bucks and being turned down. It's also America's favorite Chinese dish and is served on menus in restaurants across the country. This dish deserves GOAT status because it the first to simply combine juicy, crispy chicken in a sweet-and-sour glaze.

1 PLATE, SERVES 4 | PREP TIME: 6½ HOURS + OVERNIGHT | COOKING TIME: 1½ HOURS

INGREDIENTS
6 chicken thighs, skin on, boneless
1 cup velvet marinade (see page 70)

For the Brine
1 gallon water
1½ cups kosher salt
¾ cup sugar
2 pieces star anise

For the Sauce
1 pint water
8 ounces white sugar
1 cup rice vinegar
2 tablespoons minced garlic
2 tablespoons minced ginger

⅓ cup thin soy sauce
¼ cup black soy sauce
¼ cup oyster sauce
2 tablespoons fermented rice*
1 dried chili pepper
½ cup slurry (see page 69)

For the Batter
8 ounces cornstarch
4 ounces vegetable oil
½ cup water

For the Garnish
½ cucumber, in thinly sliced rounds
1 tablespoon sesame seeds, toasted
1 tablespoon chopped scallions

PREPARING THE CHICKEN

Let's work with chicken thighs—the most flavorful part of the bird. Leave the skin on and cut the thighs in half so the chicken pieces are large and juicy.

Next, mix all of the brine ingredients together in a large bowl. Submerge the chicken thighs in brine, cover, and let it sit in the refrigerator for 3 hours. Remove and pat dry.

Mix the velvet marinade well with a whisk. Marinate the chicken pieces in the velvet marinade for at least 3 hours, preferably overnight for maximum tenderness. Be sure to cover and store in the refrigerator. (See page 70 for velveting ingredients and technique.)

(Continued on next page)

---

* Usually sold in jars. Can be purchased online or at most Chinese supermarkets.

MAKING THE SAUCE

While you're waiting, make a deep sauce with Chinese sugar, fermented rice, rice vinegar, and a bit of chili pepper. Place all of the sauce ingredients in a pot except for slurry and stir until well-incorporated.

Place pot on high heat until it starts to simmer.

Add the slurry, reboil, check for thickness, and then remove from the heat. (Note: Watch this stage carefully. This sauce likes to boil over.)

COOKING THE CHICKEN

Set fryer to 310°F or heat oil in a wok or fry pot to that temperature. You can use a thermometer to check the oil temperature.

Mix the batter well, using the water to loosen it up. Let it sit for 3 minutes, then dip the chicken pieces in the batter.

Deep-fry the chicken pieces until the internal temperature is approximately 155°F, about 6 minutes.

Using a spider, remove the chicken pieces and let rest on a roasting rack until they come to room temperature. Meanwhile, heat the oil to 365°F.

Drop the chicken back in the fry pot until very crisp and internal temperature is at least 165°F. Remove from oil.

Separately, heat the sauce until it bubbles in a wok and, with a spider, transfer that crispy chicken into the sauce and toss.

Place the chicken on a platter with the cucumber and sprinkle some sesame seeds and scallions and you will have a classic General Tso's Chicken that everyone will love.

Tip:
There is a tiny window of time when the sauce glazes the chicken—and because of the velvet marinade and the batter being twice fried—that this dish will stay very crispy, forming four layers of texture: the crunchy coating of batter, crispy chicken skin, tender meat, and the luscious sauce that makes for a supernova of flavor with a mouthfeel that is unparalleled.

EGG ROLLS

Egg rolls are really just Chinese hot dogs with a slightly different meat, cabbage, bread, and mustard. They are rolled big with a thick wrapper and served with hot mustard and duck sauce. Similar to hot dogs—where some people like to top them with ketchup while others prefer mustard—sauce preferences for egg rolls vary based on the individual.

MAKES 6 EGG ROLLS | PREP TIME: 4 HOURS + OVERNIGHT | COOKING TIME: 7 MINUTES

INGREDIENTS

For the Filling
3 cups napa cabbage, shredded thin and lightly salted
½ cup vegetable oil
¼ cup minced garlic
¼ cup sliced white onion
24 pieces 26/30 shrimp, cleaned, shelled, deveined
½ pound roast pork, chopped (see roast pork recipe on page 129)
½ cup oyster sauce
½ cup chicken stock
½ cup soy sauce
2 tablespoons MSG
1½ cups bean sprouts

For the Wrapper
2 tablespoons all-purpose flour
2–3 tablespoons water
6 egg roll wrappers

For the Sauce
½ cup duck sauce*
½ cup Chinese mustard*

MAKING THE FILLING

Lightly salt napa cabbage and place in a colander to drain for two hours.

In large pan or wok, heat oil to medium heat. Add the garlic and onion, and cook through for 3 minutes, then increase heat to high.

Next, add the shrimp and the roast pork. Cook for 3 minutes.

Add the oyster sauce, cabbage, and chicken stock. Cook until the cabbage wilts, about 2 to 3 minutes. Once the cabbage has wilted, turn off the heat and add the soy sauce, MSG, and bean sprouts and stir.

Remove from cooking vessel, place the filling in a perforated pan or colander, and cover the mixture with plastic wrap. Place a pan on top and position a heavy can on top of that to weigh it down. This will press out all of the excess liquid and prevent the filling from weakening the wrappers, which will result in egg roll explosions when they are fried.

Place that contraption on top of a pan to catch the drippings. Let the filling chill in the refrigerator overnight.

(Continued on page 79)

★ Can be purchased online or at most Chinese supermarkets, or you can just use a couple of packets left over from your last takeout order at your local neighborhood Chinese restaurant.

WRAPPING THE EGG ROLLS

Mix the flour and water into a paste. Lay out your egg roll wrappers diagonally, so that when you're facing them, they look like diamonds. Brush the paste on the upper 3 inches of the wrapper.

Place ½ cup of filling in the lower-middle section of the diamond, fold the left and right points in, then fold the bottom half up and roll it all the way up.

COOKING PROCEDURE

Heat the oil to 325°F in your fryer pot. Fry the egg rolls until the skin is crispy and golden brown, about 6 minutes.

Transfer them to a cooling rack to rest, then plate on a platter. Serve with duck sauce and hot mustard as dipping sauces.

Watch some baseball.

Note:

There is roast pork chopped in the filling, which forces you to make the roast pork recipe found later in this book. Save some for the roast pork lo mein recipe on page 165. As you cook through this book, you will get a feel for how much roast pork means to Chinese cooking. It flows through BBQ, bao buns, fried rice, noodles, soup, and egg rolls. The great thing about Cantonese cuisine is that is that it is cumulative and reuses ingredients from other recipes, constantly building on itself.

CHICKEN CHOW MEIN

This is one of the best Chinese dishes ever. It's a super crispy pancake that soaks up a rich brown sauce into its bouncy, "noodlely" interior. Crunchy on the outside, soft and chewy on the inside; it's the noodle version of a great French bread. Yes, you will add sauce, vegetables, and chicken to finish the dish, but make no mistake—this one is all about the noodles.

MAKES 1 PLATTER, SERVES 2 | PREP TIME: 3½ HOURS + OVERNIGHT | COOKING TIME: 9 MINUTES

INGREDIENTS

4 ounces sliced chicken breast, velveted (see page 70)

¼ cup mushroom water (see page 70)

1 cup + 3 tablespoons vegetable oil (additional oil required for your fry pot; see page 71)

¼ cup salt

⅓ pound panfried or chow mein noodles

1 tablespoon minced ginger

1 tablespoon minced garlic

2 tablespoons small-diced white onion

¼ cup dried mushrooms, sliced (from mushroom water, see page 70)

¼ cup snow peas, cleaned and trimmed

½ cup chicken stock

2 tablespoons oyster sauce

2 tablespoons soy sauce

¼ cup Shaoxing wine*

1 tablespoon MSG

¼ cup slurry (see page 69)

2 tablespoons sliced scallions

¼ cup bean sprouts, washed

COOKING PROCEDURE

First, prepare the velvet marinade, submerge your chicken, cover, and let it rest for three hours or overnight in the refrigerator. Separately, prepare your mushroom water and let it rest in the refrigerator overnight. (See page 70 for velveting and mushroom water ingredients and instructions.)

Fill your blanching pot with water three-quarters of the way and set to high, then add ½ cup of oil and the salt. When the pot comes to a rolling boil, drop your noodles into the pot, and cook for 1 to 2 minutes.

Remove from the pot, strain, and place on a plate. Do not shock. Pull the noodles slightly to form a rough pancake shape, about 1 inch thick.

Next, heat a sauté pan or wok on medium heat and add ½ cup of oil to pan. Add the noodle pancake, flip when it's golden brown, about 3 to 5 minutes, and brown other side. Transfer to a shallow bowl.

Add oil to your fry pot (see page 71) and heat to 350°F. Separately, heat a sauté pan or wok to high and add 3 tablespoons of vegetable oil. Flash fry the chicken in your fry pot, then add the chicken to the sauté pan or wok until it browns, about 3 minutes. (See note about flash-frying on page 71.)

Once the chicken is browned, add the ginger, garlic, and onion, and cook through for 2 minutes. Drop in the mushrooms and snow peas, and then pour in the chicken stock. Cook for 1 minute.

Next, add the oyster sauce, soy sauce, Shaoxing wine, mushroom water, and MSG. Thicken the sauce by adding the slurry.

Top the noodle pancake with vegetables, chicken, and sauce. Garnish the whole dish with scallions and bean sprouts.

★ Can be purchased online or at most Chinese supermarkets.

BEEF AND BROCCOLI

A meat and vegetable never paired better. Rich slices of velveted beef combined with hearty Chinese broccoli sautéed in oyster sauce reaches savory levels that few dishes can match.

Chinese broccoli is a hearty vegetable that has a slightly bitter, earthy flavor that is the perfect addition to this dish. Its fibrous stem is a vivid contrast to its velvety leaves, which can make it seem like it is actually two different types of vegetables in one. The leaves also are a fraction of the width of the stems but can stand up to high-heat cooking. With its distinct taste and unique characteristics, it adds great texture and complements many different flavor profiles.

Despite its name, this dish is actually a trio, as it's brought together with oyster sauce, which meets the saltiness of soy with a blast of savory flavor, joining together in a perfect harmonious blend. This recipe is a perfect example of how deeper flavors are formed by utilizing preserved foods in our cuisine.

1 PLATTER, SERVES 2 | PREP TIME: 30 MINUTES + OVERNIGHT | COOKING TIME: 8 MINUTES

INGREDIENTS

6-ounce flank steak, sliced thin on the bias, velveted (see page 70)

¼ cup mushroom water (see page 70)

3 tablespoons vegetable oil

1 tablespoon minced garlic

½ tablespoon minced ginger

2 tablespoons diced white onion

4 stalks Chinese broccoli,† sliced, blanched, and shocked

½ cup oyster sauce

¼ cup soy sauce

¼ cup Shaoxing wine*

½ tablespoon MSG

2 tablespoons slurry (see page 69)

¼ cup fried shallots,* slightly crushed

COOKING PROCEDURE

Marinate your beef in the velvet marinade overnight. Separately, prepare your mushroom water and let it rest in the refrigerator overnight. (See page 70 for velveting and mushroom water ingredients and instructions.)

Heat the fry pot to 350°F and your separate wok or pot to medium heat. (See note about flash-frying on page 71.)

Add 3 tablespoons of vegetable oil to your pan or wok and drop in the garlic, ginger, and onion, cooking through for 2 minutes. Then add broccoli and toss with all of the aromatics.

Meanwhile, drop your beef into the spider and lower it into the fry pot. Lift your spider out of the bubbling oil after 10 seconds, shake it carefully, and add the beef to the pan or wok with the Chinese broccoli.

Toss everything together, then add the oyster sauce and soy sauce, and reduce the mixture slightly for 2 minutes. Add the Shaoxing wine, mushroom water, and MSG, and reduce for another 2 minutes. Incorporate the slurry to thicken the sauce.

Remove from heat and serve on a platter. Top with fried shallots.

---

† A close substitute is broccoli rabe.

* Can be purchased online or at most Chinese supermarkets.

SWEET-AND-SOUR PORK, PEKING STYLE

My family and I order this dish all the time, as it is common in the kitchens of Chinatown. It has A.1. Steak Sauce in it, so it's somewhat of an American hybrid. What it isn't is your prototypical sweet-and-sour pork. This dish features juicy pork chops on the bone with a pungent glaze. It's the Chinese American version of sweet-and-sour pork.

1 PLATTER, SERVES 2 | PREP TIME: 5 HOURS + OVERNIGHT | COOKING TIME: 15 MINUTES

INGREDIENTS

For Brining the Pork Chops
1 gallon water
1½ cups kosher salt
¾ cup sugar
2 pieces star anise
6 pork chops, thinly sliced

For the Savory Marinade
1 cup oyster sauce
¼ cup soy sauce
¼ cup Shaoxing wine*
¼ cup sugar
2 cloves garlic, crushed
3 tablespoons hoisin sauce

For the Velvet Marinade (see page 70)
4 ounces cornstarch
2 eggs
2 tablespoons Shaoxing wine*
1 teaspoon baking soda

For the Sauce
1 ounce A.1. Steak Sauce
½ ounce Worcestershire sauce
1½ ounces Chinese red vinegar*
1 ounce Chinkiang vinegar
4 ounces sugar
3 tablespoons honey
⅓ cup water
¼ cup slurry (see page 69)

For the Garnishes
1 scallion, sliced
2 tablespoons minced ginger
1 tablespoon sesame seeds

★ Can be purchased online or at most Chinese supermarkets.

COOKING PROCEDURE

Brining and Marinating the Pork Chops

Mix all the brine ingredients together, then add the pork chops and leave in the brine for 2 hours in your refrigerator.

Mix all the savory marinade ingredients together in a separate container. After it finishes brining, transfer the pork chops to the savory marinade and refrigerate for 3 hours.

Next, mix the velvet marinade ingredients together well with a whisk. Transfer pork chops from savory marinade to velvet marinade and place in the refrigerator overnight.

For the Sauce

Mix all of the sauce ingredients, except for the slurry, together in a pot. Bring the sauce to a boil and thicken with the slurry. Reserve.

Cooking the Pork Chops

Heat your fry pot to 350°F. You can check the oil with a thermometer. See flash-frying technique on page 71. Once the oil is the proper temperature, flash-fry the pork chops until 165°F, about 4 minutes.

Next, heat 2 cups of the sauce in a separate pan until it's bubbling, transfer pork chops to the pan with sauce, toss the chops in the sauce, and then transfer to a platter.

Garnish with scallion, ginger, and sesame seeds.

CHAPTER 6

VEGETABLES

In 1997, I started working at Jean-Georges, the two-star Michelin restaurant in Manhattan. I had the honor of being part of the crew that earned four stars from the *New York Times* in its first year of opening.

I was head of the vegetable station and all I did was cook vegetables every day, keeping them bright green, cutting to uniform sizes, and developing superior knife skills along the way. My job was to blanch and shock vegetables for my station. You would test the doneness by time, color, and tasting, trying a piece here and there as you cooked to make sure they were done right.

You focused only on cooking. For the time you worked at a restaurant like this, the job is so hard and the hours so long, that you had no choice but to immerse yourself into the life of four-star cooking. Silence in this kitchen, unless you were telling chef your plate would be up in thirty seconds. It was the hardest job I ever had, and also the place where I learned the most in the least amount of time.

I had never cooked French food, and although I had worked for Jean-Georges

Vongerichten previously at Vong, this was a very different kitchen. The bar was so high and the cooking so intense, no one cared what you did before; they expected you to be a killer from the first service.

I started off a bit behind, and it took a while to get up to speed. I fell from grace many times to the point I wanted to give up. Once you have that target on your back in a kitchen like that, there is not much hope for you. My cooking was not on the same level as my fellow cooks and it was transparent to everyone, all the way up the ranks right to Jean-Georges himself, who was there every day and with whom I spent many mornings cooking.

Cooking with him may seem awesome, and looking back on it, it certainly was, but at the time it was painful. The way to fully learning your craft in those kitchens at that time was through a militaristic process of breaking you down until you saw the light.

It was there that I had the single worst night of my career. The James Beard House's top board members were booked for dinner and the restaurant that night was completely reserved. I had nothing prepped by the start of service, and at about 6:00 p.m. the ticket machine started to spit out dupes with the night's first orders. I may have had a mild heart attack at that point. I had to cook almost everything to order, and was ten minutes late on every dish. I had other cooks and sous-chefs coming to help me out just for their own survival.

However, that night turned out to be one of the best of my life.

During that service, I discovered a nugget of wisdom about vegetable cooking that I still carry deep inside of me to this day. By focusing on the cooking I found the sweet spot for preparing vegetables—the perfect cooking time—and it was a beautiful thing.

There is approximately a five-second window when cooking vegetables, where they will yield a sweet taste and texture that's close to perfection. As you bite, you will forget there is anything else on this earth but that perfect vegetable. A few seconds more and that snow pea or haricot vert is still good, but not perfect. It's 96 percent. You would think that that last 4 percent isn't important, but it's a tremendous gulf. It means the world, especially when you're cooking at that level.

To this day, I compare every vegetable I cook to those from that day, when I first found the sweet spot. It inspired me and gave me my station, my job, and kitchen cred. My cooking improved, clarified. It was a crossroad, and it ushered me into a whole new world of cooking.

Cooking in the Countryside

Later in my career, I was fortunate enough to cook in China. Not in a restaurant, but on a farm in the countryside of Shenjiamen, a string of islands off the coast of Shanghai. We prepared dinners helping my wife's family cook banquets for special occasions for their village.

It was as country as you can get. I sliced my vegetables on a cutting board that was actually a shredded piece of wood. There were two sources of water: one pipe that was shared by several houses and the lake. If outhouses were to come back in vogue, this place would be trending. I got to see rolling hills of nothing but green rice paddies, the family's crab farm, and the local markets.

We always cooked dinner in the morning and I often wondered why. As I took a good look at the kitchen, I found there weren't any light fixtures. I realized that once it got dark, you couldn't cook.

We picked our scallions and radishes from the farm just a few feet away from the kitchen; killed and de-feathered the chickens for braising; went down to the dock to get fish that were caught just hours before; and prepared it all on a bamboo-fueled wok. None of the food ever saw the inside of a refrigerator. That is farm-to-table (and ocean-to-table) cooking. There is something that stirs in your soul when you eat a meal cooked like that. That is, if you are a chef from New York City. For everybody else, it was dinner.

Rooted in My Brain

I remember all those great times cooking when I walk down the vegetable aisles in the supermarkets of Chinatown. It's those memories that have been buried deep into my brain and will sound a subconscious "alarm" when I veer from the disciplines of cooking.

I look at vegetables through those two lenses, filtered through all the great food I've eaten all my life—the sautéed watercress on the menu in Chinatown, fermented tofu with string beans at home, and all the bok choy I've cooked in my kitchens.

The technical skills needed to create great vegetable dishes, the enjoyment of eating them, a firsthand appreciation of how they are grown, and the deep connection they have to us as a community are all central to the way I think about vegetables.

Thinking back to my childhood, my grandmother could be just as strict in the kitchen as Jean-Georges, and she would be just as picky with her ingredients, always demanding things like vegetables be the freshest and most flavorful, at their peak, and would buy only enough for the night's dinner.

CUCUMBER SALAD

I used to believe that there were no salads in Chinese cuisine. At least in the southern part of China, the common belief is that raw greens are for feeding farm animals. Then I ate a plate of marinated Sichuan cucumbers. Refreshing, light, and full of bold flavors, this salad hits the spot on a hot summer day. I now love Chinese salads, and I'm not an animal. (Well, not a farm animal.)

1 PLATTER, SERVES 2 | PREP TIME: 3½ HOURS | COOKING TIME: 2 MINUTES

INGREDIENTS
1 English cucumber
1 tablespoon kosher salt

For the Dressing
½ cup Chinkiang vinegar
1 tablespoon white sugar
1 tablespoon dark soy sauce
1 tablespoon mushroom
    soy sauce
½ shallot, minced
½ clove garlic, minced
½ tablespoon minced ginger
1 dry chili, minced
½ piece star anise
1 tablespoon sesame oil
3 tablespoons vegetable oil
1 teaspoon MSG
½ tablespoon ground bean
    sauce (*Koon Chun*)*

Finishing Touches
1 finger ginger, peeled,
    julienned
6 cherry tomatoes, sliced
    in half
1 tablespoon chili oil* (see
    page 39 to make your own)

COOKING PROCEDURE

For the Cucumbers
Peel off the skin of the cucumber every ½ inch, yielding a stripe design on the cucumber. Cut in half lengthwise, scoop out the seeds, then slice ½-inch segments.

Place the cucumber in a large bowl, sprinkle in the salt, and toss. Cover bowl with plastic wrap and chill 2 hours. (This will release excess water from the cucumber. The liquid is very flavorful, but salty.)

For the Dressing
Combine all dressing ingredients in a mixing bowl. Mix thoroughly, cover, and let it rest for 1 hour.

The star anise can be removed prior to dressing the cucumbers. Place the salted cucumbers (you can discard the cucumber water or save for another use) and submerge them in the dressing. Let it sit in the refrigerator for 30 minutes to chill.

Finishing Touches
Heat your fry pot (a deep pan or stockpot) to 330°F, drop your julienned ginger, and fry until brown and crispy. Remove from the oil and transfer to a paper towel–lined plate. Blot off any excess oil.

Transfer your marinated cucumbers to a serving platter. Top with fried ginger and cherry tomatoes. Add chili oil to taste, or serve on the side. Note: If you are making your own chili oil, add a day to your prep time.

---

* This can be found online or at most Chinese supermarkets.

SAUTÉED BOK CHOY

As previously mentioned, there are many varieties of bok choy at the market, and it's your job to shop, pick what you like, find what looks and tastes best, and to go home and cook it. Then go back and try another kind. I personally love Shanghai bok choy. Those little jade green buttery bulbs of sweetness are perfect size for cooking and require very little preparation. This may be the simplest recipe in the book, but that means your vegetables and aromatics should be cut fresh and at their height of flavor. Focus on the cooking to find that sweet spot for your bok choy.

1 PLATTER, SERVES 2 | PREP TIME: 15 MINUTES + OVERNIGHT | COOKING TIME: 8 MINUTES

INGREDIENTS

¼ cup mushroom water (see page 70)

5 pieces Shanghai bok choy, washed

3 tablespoons vegetable oil

¼ white onion, thinly sliced

1 tablespoon minced garlic

½ tablespoon peeled and minced ginger

¼ cup Shaoxing wine*

2 tablespoons thin soy sauce

1 tablespoon mushroom soy sauce

½ tablespoon MSG

GARNISHES

1 tablespoon fried garlic, slightly crushed

2 tablespoons thinly sliced scallions

COOKING PROCEDURE

First, prepare your mushroom water (see page 70) and let it rest in the refrigerator overnight.

Split your bok choy in half and remove the core.

Heat pan or wok on medium heat and add the vegetable oil. Add the onion, then the garlic and the ginger, and cook for 2 minutes.

Next drop in your bok choy and turn heat to high. Pour in the Shaoxing wine and cook for 1 minute.

Add both soy sauces and mushroom water, turn the bok choy over and cover pan, then reduce the cooking liquid slightly, about 2 to 3 minutes.

Remove cover, add MSG, and stir. (You can add a slurry if you want the liquid to thicken; I prefer this to be brothy.)

Remove and transfer to a platter. Top with fried garlic and scallions.

---

* Can be purchased online or at most Chinese supermarkets.

STIR-FRIED EGGPLANT

All the recipes in this chapter are vegetarian. If you are a vegetarian or vegan, China celebrates this lifestyle. Chinese culture has a huge Buddhist sect who follow a strict vegetarian diet, so it is important to me to keep the vegetarian integrity of these vegetable dishes. I love to celebrate Chinese vegetables and cook them without the addition of meat and seafood, but many of our sauces and condiments make it difficult to cook entirely vegetarian.

This particular dish needs oyster sauce, but now, thankfully, there are vegetarian options. There is even a gluten-free oyster sauce, but there is not yet a vegetarian gluten-free version. I submitted a request to Lee Kum Kee and even received a sample product, but they have not offered anything official yet. I'll bet something is on the way. You can, of course, use standard oyster sauce, too, but just know Buddha is watching.

1 PLATTER, SERVES 2 | PREP TIME: 20 MINUTES | COOKING TIME: 8 MINUTES

INGREDIENTS
¼ cup vegetable oil

2 whole shallots, peeled and sliced

1 tablespoon minced garlic

2 Chinese eggplants, cut into quarters, then into 1-inch segments, yielding triangle cuts

10 dried shiitake mushrooms (reconstituted in cold water overnight)

¼ cup vegetarian oyster sauce

¼ cup Shaoxing wine*

2 tablespoons thin soy sauce

1 tablespoon mushroom soy sauce

1 tablespoon dark soy sauce

1 dried chili pepper, crushed

½ cup cherry tomatoes, halfed

½ cup slurry (see page 69)

1 large knob ginger, peeled and julienned

2 scallions, sliced

2 tablespoons chopped cilantro

½ lime

COOKING PROCEDURE

Heat pan to medium heat and add vegetable oil. Add the shallots and garlic and cook for 2 minutes.

Drop in the eggplant and the mushrooms and turn the heat to high. Add the vegetarian oyster sauce, Shaoxing wine, and all three of the soy sauces. Cook for 1 minute. Add dried chili pepper and the tomatoes and stir in.

Incorporate the slurry to thicken the sauce and then transfer to a plate or dish. Be generous topping the dish with the ginger, scallions, and cilantro. Serve with lime.

Tip:
Cut your eggplants last or they will quickly discolor without some acid like lime or lemon juice. Your knife, of course, will always be clean, but it needs to be especially clean when cutting eggplant because eggplant will absorb everything.

---

* Can be purchased online or at most Chinese supermarkets.

OLD-SCHOOL CHINATOWN VEGETABLES

All my life, I have eaten in Chinese restaurants. From Chinatown classics to small takeout joints in Brooklyn, the occasional banquet in midtown to the big suburban dining rooms in Jersey: they all serve a selection of vegetables that most of us can identify as "Chinese food vegetables." Whether you knew it was canned or not, the baby corn, mushrooms, bamboo shoots, and water chestnuts that appeared on platters coming out of the kitchen always stood out, either because you didn't know what bamboo shoots were or you were amazed by the baby corn being, well, baby corn.

This is the Bionic Man of vegetable dishes. With little effort, we can rebuild this. We have the technology. We have the capability to make this dish better . . . fresher . . . tastier. All of these ingredients can be bought from the Chinese market fresh. Use some vegetarian oyster sauce and it will take you back to those days as a kid in the Chinese restaurant. Only this time, you will love all the vegetables—not just the baby corn.

1 PLATTER, SERVES 2 | PREP TIME: 30 MINUTES + OVERNIGHT | COOKING TIME: 8 MINUTES

INGREDIENTS
½ cup mushroom water (see page 70)
3 tablespoons vegetable oil
¼ cup white onion, thinly sliced
½ tablespoon minced ginger
1 tablespoon minced garlic
½ cup fresh baby corn, sliced on bias into bite-sized portions
¼ cup fresh water chestnuts, cleaned and sliced in half
½ piece fresh bamboo shoot, rinsed and sliced to bite size
½ cup snow peas, cleaned and trimmed
¼ cup Shaoxing wine*
¼ cup sliced king oyster mushrooms
¼ cup sliced shiitake mushrooms
¼ cup vegetarian oyster sauce
¼ cup thin soy sauce
2 tablespoons mushroom soy sauce
1 tablespoon MSG
½ cup slurry (see page 69)

COOKING PROCEDURE
First, prepare your mushroom water (see page 70) and let it rest in the refrigerator overnight.

Heat a pan or wok to medium heat and add vegetable oil. Add the onion, ginger, and garlic, and cook through for 2 minutes.

Increase the heat to high and add baby corn, water chestnuts, bamboo shoot, snow peas, and both types of mushrooms, cooking for about 2 minutes. Incorporate the Shaoxing wine, mushroom water, vegetarian oyster sauce, thin soy sauce, mushroom soy sauce, and MSG, and cook for another 2 minutes. Bring the mixture a boil, then add the slurry to thicken the sauce.

Transfer to a platter and serve.

> ### Tip:
> While you can use a canned substitute for many recipes in this book, it is infinitely preferable that all of the vegetables in this recipe are fresh because, duh, the point of this dish is to use fresh vegetables in place of the canned ones used in so many Chinese restaurants.

---

* Can be purchased online or at most Chinese supermarkets.

THREE CUPS CAULIFLOWER

This dish is a variation of the classic "Three Cups Chicken." The addition of chilies, basil, and cilantro in this rich sauce shows off the great nuances that can push the envelope in Chinese cooking. Those aromatics really give the dish a blast that fresh herbs rarely get to do when eaten on the mainland. The cauliflower soaks it all up in a way that makes chickens all over the world a little happier.

1 PLATTER, SERVES 4 | PREP TIME: 20 MINUTES + OVERNIGHT | COOKING TIME 30 MINUTES

INGREDIENTS

½ cup mushroom water (see page 70)
1 tablespoon vegetable oil
1 white onion, thinly sliced
2 cloves garlic, minced
1 cup thin soy sauce
1 cup Shaoxing wine*
½ cup sesame oil
3 tablespoons Chinese sugar*
1 head of cauliflower, stem cut out stem chopped into florets
1 finger ginger, peeled and minced
1 chili pepper, Thai or jalapeño, thinly sliced
¼ cup slurry (see page 69)
¼ cup cilantro, minced
8 Thai basil leaves
Jasmine rice, for plating

COOKING PROCEDURE

First, prepare your mushroom water (see page 70) and let it rest in the refrigerator overnight.

Heat your wok on medium heat with the vegetable oil. Add the onion and cook for 2 minutes, then add the garlic.

Next, add the soy sauce, Shaoxing wine, sesame oil, mushroom water, and sugar, and let simmer for 20 minutes, which should reduce it by 25 percent.

Add the cauliflower, ginger, and chili pepper and simmer for 10 more minutes until the sauce is slightly thick and cauliflower is cooked.

Add slurry and bring back to a boil, then add the cilantro and basil. Take off the fire and place everything in a serving bowl. Serve with jasmine rice.

★ Can be purchased online or at most Chinese supermarkets.

SICHUAN VEGETABLES

For those who have experienced the joys of eating dried chilies mixed with Sichuan peppercorn, it's not just a slap of flavors; it's a smack that will numb your whole mouth, maybe even your whole being. It is an experience that alters your state of mind with a little help from a couple shots of baijiu (the booze of China).

Many people already know about the fun of eating Sichuan food. People tell me all the time that they can't eat Chinese food because it's too spicy and it blows my mind that the only Chinese food they were introduced to is Sichuan, not Cantonese or even Shanghainese.

However, there is greatness in this cuisine. You can see this in a humble bowl of vegetables enhanced by those chilies and peppercorns, the red hue of the sauce rising to the top. Take in all the aromatics as they fill the air.

In Sichuan cooking, the garlic reacts to the sugar and the vinegar in a way so differently than its brother and sister cuisines from southern China. Those bold and bright flavors have to find a way to cut through and balance all that spicy numbness.

1 PLATTER, SERVES 2 | PREP TIME: 2 HOURS | COOKING TIME: 10 MINUTES

INGREDIENTS

For the Sichuan Sauce
1 tablespoon vegetable oil
1 tablespoon minced garlic
1 tablespoon minced fresh hot peppers
  (Thai chilies* or jalapeño)
½ tablespoon crushed dried chili pepper
½ tablespoon ground Sichuan peppercorns
½ cup hoisin sauce
3 tablespoons thin soy sauce
2 tablespoon sweet soy sauce
1 tablespoon ground bean paste*
2 tablespoons sugar
1 tablespoon sherry cooking wine
2 tablespoons Shaoxing wine*
1 tablespoon Chinkiang vinegar
2 tablespoons white vinegar
1 tablespoon Chinese red vinegar*
1 tablespoon sesame oil
¾ cup slurry (see page 69)

For the Vegetables
¼ cup vegetable oil
¼ white onion, sliced
2 tablespoons minced garlic
2 tablespoons peeled and minced ginger
½ tablespoon dry chili peppers, slightly crushed,
  flash-fried
½ tablespoon Sichuan peppercorns, slightly crushed
¼ cup snow peas, cleaned and trimmed
¼ cup string beans, cleaned and trimmed
1 cup water spinach, bottom stem trimmed and cut to
  2-inch pieces
¼ cup deseeded thinly sliced red bell peppers
8 mushrooms (dried or fresh), sliced in half
1 cup Sichuan sauce*
2 tablespoons Shaoxing wine
1 tablespoon MSG
¼ cup shelled peanuts, slightly crushed, flash-fried
1 scallion, sliced

(Continued on next page)

★ Can be purchased online or at most Chinese supermarkets.

COOKING PROCEDURE

For the Sichuan Sauce

Place a sauce pot on medium heat and add the vegetable oil.

Add garlic, hot peppers, chilies, crushed dried chili pepper, and peppercorns, cooking through until soft, about 2 to 3 minutes.

Next, incorporate hoisin sauce, soy sauces, ground bean paste, sugar, and the sherry and Shaoxing wines. Bring the mixture to a boil.

Finally, add the vinegars and sesame oil. Bring back to a boil and add the slurry to thicken the sauce. Reserve.

For the Vegetables

Heat a pan or wok on medium heat with the vegetable oil. Add the onion, garlic, and ginger, and cook through for 3 minutes.

Next, drop in the crushed dried chilies and peppercorns. Cook for 1 minute. Then add the vegetables and mushrooms. Stir well, cooking until soft, about 3 minutes.

Pour in the Sichuan sauce, Shaoxing wine, and MSG. Bring to a simmer.

Remove from pan and transfer to a platter. Top with peanuts and garnish with sliced scallion.

WATERCRESS WITH BLACK BEAN GARLIC SAUCE

This is a great go-to recipe for most vegetables, and goes well with water spinach, regular or baby spinach, watercress, or all the above. Take a good look at many Chinese restaurant menus, and you will notice that although it may look like there are way too many selections, the same preparations are used for many different main ingredients. Black bean garlic sauce is one of the mother preparations that can be used for all kinds of seafood and meat dishes and, of course, vegetables.

1 PLATTER, SERVES 4 | PREP TIME: 20 MINUTES | COOKING TIME: 5 MINUTES

INGREDIENTS
2 tablespoons vegetable oil

3 tablespoons diced white onion

1½ tablespoons coarsely chopped garlic

½ tablespoon peeled and minced ginger

1 tablespoon fermented black beans,* washed, patted dry, and crushed into a paste

2 bunches watercress

2 tablespoons thin soy sauce

1½ tablespoon vegetarian oyster sauce

1 tablespoon Shaoxing wine*

½ tablespoon sesame oil

1 tablespoon mushroom soy sauce

½ tablespoon MSG

1 pinch white pepper

1 tablespoon fried garlic

COOKING PROCEDURE

Heat wok to medium and add the vegetable oil. When the pan is hot, add the onion and garlic, and cook for 2 minutes.

Next, add the ginger, fermented black bean paste, and watercress, cooking for 1 minute.

Then incorporate the thin soy sauce, vegetarian oyster sauce, Shaoxing wine, sesame oil, and mushroom soy sauce, and cook until watercress is fully wilted.

Add the MSG and white pepper and stir in for 30 seconds. Transfer to a serving platter and top with fried garlic.

> ## Tip:
> If there are no allergy concerns, this is a good time to try cooking with peanut oil instead of vegetable oil. Old-school cooks used to use this stronger oil to cook with, which imparted a distinct flavor to all their recipes. Take the DeLorean and head back to a simpler, *peanuttier* time of cooking.

* Can be purchased online or at most Chinese supermarkets.

CHAPTER 7

FISH AND SEAFOOD

The eastern coast of China is big. What's in the ocean that runs alongside it defines the cuisine there. The cooking explores every facet, level, and way you can coax flavor out of an ocean creature. Chinese people invented the "seafood time stop," where we dry and preserve it in its current state and concentrate its flavors. From there, the cooking possibilities are endless.

A long time ago, someone had the thought: *Why don't we save our bounty of seafood so it doesn't go to waste, and when winter comes we don't have to go out and freeze while chasing the fish? We could . . . like . . . preserve our catch now, and eat all winter.* That guy could have starved to death, but probably wound up saving humanity.

The use of dried scallops, shrimp, oysters, and fish show up in so many places in Chinese cooking that you may as well expect it to be in every dish, snack, or food that you eat. Be surprised if it isn't. That's how much Chinese people love fish and seafood. You will find it everywhere in Hong Kong, Fujian, Beijing, Shanghai, and in Chinatown.

If I'm talking about my perspective of cooking seafood through the lens of Chinese cuisine, I could not leave out the time I spent in Shenjiamen.

Located off the coast of Shanghai, Shenjiamen is one of the largest fishing ports in China. Fish and seafood are its natural resources. According to the fishermen I met there, the port is responsible for about 10 percent of all the commercial fishing in all of China. Fish and seafood hanging in the sun to dry is a typical scene in everyday life, and it's hung all over the place—in front of houses, in hallways, on rooftops.

The first dish I ate there was at my wife's grandmother's house, and the meal was prepared specially for our arrival. She was so happy to serve a traditional dish for occasions like homecomings. It was a simple, rustic plate of fish served over rice. The fish was soft and slightly pungent, and it was preserved. The preservation technique used to make this dish was a true home-cooking marvel that, as a chef, I truly respected.

The fish was scaled and covered with rice wine, and placed in a clay pot and stored

Fish drying in the sun in Shenjiamen, China.

in a kitchen cabinet for three months. There were other small details, but in essence, that was it. If she had known we were coming earlier she would have preserved it for three more months, which would have made the bones soft enough to eat. That's sustainability like I never had seen before. It was the real stuff. These were lessons in medieval cooking, in birth-of-civilization cooking. You can't find this stuff on Tripadvisor.

This dish left me in awe of the history that must have accompanied it. How many generations did it feed to get to us at this moment? How long did it take for this dish to transition from a food necessary for survival to a traditional dish served as a badge of honor for its origins? It was a window to cooking a thousand years ago when Chinese cuisine was just a baby and its momma was the Pacific Ocean.

Mastery of seafood cookery was a by-product of survival. That's how a cuisine starts, evolves, and perfects itself. This stuff doesn't just taste good. It tastes deep, blessed, and timeless. It's a beautiful thing to love something that shouldn't taste good but does because it's been a part of your culture for a very long time. It's like the Japanese *nattō*, that fermented ammonia shark dish in Iceland, or cheese.

That preserved fish is now presented as a dish of celebration, knowing it takes three to six months to prepare. It is now only served to make people happy, and its techniques have been passed on to chefs and cooks to expand on it however they like. There is magic here, and I hope you see it, too. When you cook, know that this is the soul-stirring part of our cuisine, the defining part, the start of it all.

STEAMED PRESERVED SALTED FISH

This is a simple but intensely delicious dish that contains bits of history, survival, and (of course) salt. If you aren't used to the aroma it will give off when it cooks, you'd better get ready. It is potent. When you bite into it, a complex salt burst enters your mouth that is comprised of the concentrated flavor of the fish itself and rides the ginger and scallion to a savory and satisfying finish. There will be bones, smells, facial puckering, and happiness.

The dish has never changed, Chinese people know it and love it for exactly what it is. This recipe plainly shows off the simple affinity Chinese people have for preserved foods. It has no sauce and is meant to be accompanied by other foods in your bowl of rice to offset its intense salty flavor. Occasionally, you will scoop a bite of the fish into your mouth and it will be like the first time Jim Ignatowski ate that brownie.

1 PLATTER, SERVES 4 | PREP TIME: 10 MINUTES | COOKING TIME: 15 MINUTES

INGREDIENTS
1 salted yellow croaker*
1 finger ginger, peeled
   and julienned
1 scallion, sliced

COOKING PROCEDURE
Set your bamboo steamer to high and transfer your fish to a plate.

Place the plate inside steamer for approximately 15 minutes. You are looking for softness, as the salt has already transformed the protein and the fish is no longer technically raw.

Remove the plate from steamer, and top the dish with ginger and scallion.

Serve with bowls of jasmine rice.

★ Can be purchased online or at most Chinese supermarkets.

CHAR SUI BLACK COD

I discovered black cod when I cooked for Nobu Matsuhisa at his original Tribeca restaurant years ago. His Saikyo Miso Cod dish became a global phenomenon, and I was proud to have had a hand in it. As part of the opening kitchen crew, I was given the responsibility early on of butchering the fish, making the marinade, and cooking it to order on the line. So I know this fish very well. We must have sold thousands over the years. Flaky, sweet, savory, this dish's ability to absorb big flavors make it a thing of beauty. Of course, in a reverse Asian twist, I made it a Chinese dish later in my career. It's not traditional, but it's still damn good.

1 PLATTER, SERVES 2 | PREP TIME: 2½ HOURS + OVERNIGHT | COOKING TIME: 12 MINUTES

INGREDIENTS
¼ cup kosher salt
7-ounce fillet of black cod, skin on (see tip below)

FOR THE MARINADE
2 tablespoons white onion, diced
1 tablespoon minced garlic
½ tablespoon peeled and minced ginger
½ cup hoisin sauce
1 tablespoon ground bean sauce (Koon Chun)*
2 tablespoons soy sauce
½ tablespoon sesame oil
¼ cup Shaoxing wine*
½ tablespoon Chinese five-spice powder
3 tablespoons honey
2 tablespoons white sugar
2 pieces fermented black bean,* washed and patted dry, slightly crushed

FINISHING TOUCHES
1 tablespoon vegetable oil
½ tablespoon minced garlic
2 pieces Shanghai bok choy, cut in half, washed, dried
1 tablespoon soy sauce
¼ cup Shaoxing wine*
1 tablespoon thinly sliced scallion
½ tablespoon peeled and minced ginger
1 tablespoon cilantro, minced

Tip:
Black cod is also called sablefish. If it's not available, the best substitute is Chilean sea bass.

* Can be purchased online or at most Chinese supermarkets.

COOKING PROCEDURE

Sprinkle salt on both sides of the fish, wrap with plastic wrap, and place in the refrigerator for 2 hours.

Make the marinade by combining all the marinade ingredients in a pot and bringing to a boil, then remove from the fire and set aside until it reaches room temperature.

Submerge the fish into the marinade and return to the refrigerator in a covered container overnight.

The next day, remove the fish from the marinade and gently shake off any excess marinade. Heat your oven to 450°F.

Place in a sauté or sizzle pan and put in the oven for 10 minutes. Heat a sauté pan on medium and add your vegetable oil. Add the garlic to the pan and cook for 1 minute.

Next, add the bok choy and cook for 2 minutes, then incorporate the soy sauce and Shaoxing wine, cooking for an additional 2 minutes.

Transfer the bok choy to a platter with a little of the cooking broth. Top with the fish.

Garnish with scallion, ginger, and cilantro.

BLACK BEAN CLAMS

This dish is a Cantonese classic. Seared clams in the shell are hit with the funkiness of fermented black beans. Whoever made these beans gave a culinary treasure to Chinese cooking. Add a couple of them here and there to a stir-fry and it will put that dish over the top. Make a dish with black bean garlic sauce and you venture into the best of Chinese cooking.

1 PLATTER, SERVES 2 | PREP TIME: 20 MINUTES | COOKING TIME: 8 MINUTES

INGREDIENTS

¼ cup vegetable oil

2 tablespoons minced garlic

1 tablespoon peeled and minced ginger

2 tablespoons finely chopped red bell pepper

24 littleneck clams, scrubbed clean

1 cup Shaoxing wine*

1 cup chicken stock

1 tablespoon oyster sauce

1½ tablespoons fermented black beans,* soaked and patted dry, chopped fine

1 tablespoon thin soy sauce

½ tablespoon Chinese sugar

1 pinch white pepper

½ tablespoon sesame oil

1 tablespoon MSG

½ cup slurry (see page 69)

2 tablespoons scallions, sliced

COOKING PROCEDURE

Heat wok or pan to medium heat and add vegetable oil. Add garlic, ginger, and bell pepper, cooking through for 3 minutes.

Turn the heat in your pan to high, add the clams, and toss.

Next, add the Shaoxing wine, chicken stock, oyster sauce, fermented black beans, thin soy sauce, Chinese sugar, white pepper, sesame oil, and MSG. Stir, cover, and cook for 2 minutes. Add slurry and bring to a boil to thicken the sauce.

When the clams open, toss them in the sauce and transfer to a serving platter with sauce. Garnish with scallions.

Tip:

Clams don't follow the clock. They open when they want to, and never open at the same time. Cooking clams in the shell demands an experienced sense of timing. Also, keep in mind that there is no substitute for the liquid that escapes from the clams. However, you can cheat a bit and steam the clams first, reserve what you can of the liquid, and cook it all in the sauce so they are all cooked uniformly and everything comes out consistent. If they don't open, don't eat them.

---

* Can be purchased online or at most Chinese supermarkets.

SALT-AND-PEPPER SHRIMP

This is a great snack that I have seen made with small shrimps, huge prawns, and every size in between. In New York City, the seasons for live shrimp are short, so choose your frozen shrimp with a discerning eye or wait for the shrimps to turn up in those tanks. Despite this important detail, if you can get great-quality shrimp, this snack combines things that are usually irresistible, especially with a cold beer after work. Seafood, frying, and salt make this our gift to the beer gods.

1 PLATTER, SERVES 2 | PREP TIME: 20 MINUTES | COOKING TIME: 6 MINUTES

INGREDIENTS

For the Five-Spice Seasoning Mixture
½ cup kosher salt

1 tablespoon MSG

1 tablespoon Chinese five-spice powder

1 teaspoon dried chili, crushed

1 teaspoon cardamom seed, crushed (it's not traditional, but it adds some zing to the salt mix)

For the Shrimp
12 16/20 shrimp, shell on, head on, deveined

½ cup cornstarch

1 tablespoon minced garlic

½ tablespoon peeled and minced ginger

1 tablespoon Thai chili or jalapeño, thinly sliced

1 tablespoon fried garlic

1 scallion, sliced

COOKING PROCEDURE

For the Five-Spice Seasoning Mixture
Combine the salt, MSG, five-spice powder, dried chili, and cardamom. Mix thoroughly.

For the Shrimp
Heat oil to 325°F in your fry pot.

Dredge the shrimp in cornstarch and shake off any excess. Carefully drop shrimp in the oil and fry for 2 to 3 minutes.

Heat wok to high and add the shrimp, the five-spice seasoning mixture, garlic, ginger, and Thai chili or jalapeño pepper. Toss everything together for about 1 to 2 minutes.

Remove to a serving platter and top with fried garlic and scallion. Enjoy with a beer.

Tip:
The shell and head are typically left on, but if you are sensitive to that, you can remove those. However, that would be like watching TV without the sound or listening to a Led Zeppelin song without the drums ("Moby Dick," specifically). When the slightly chewy shell starts to melt in your mouth and the salt hits your taste buds and mixes with the remnants of the hot fry oil, you enter into a seafood-eating frenzy, pulling off the head with your teeth and sucking out all those juices and guts.

CRISPY FISH MAPO TOFU

Mapo tofu is a unique, beautiful dish that celebrates tofu. Tofu is often stigmatized as a health food that has no taste and the texture of mush, which makes it completely misunderstood in American culture. There is no such feeling toward tofu in Chinese cuisine and here is why: Tofu has a hidden superpower. It's a steroid for texture and flavor.

In this dish that combines two iconic dishes, the soft, lush tofu plays off the crispy texture of the flaky, sweet, chili-spiked fish fillet, and is all brought together by the natural spiciness of the mapo seasonings. Add fatty pork to the mix, infuse it with the bold, spicy, and deep flavors of Sichuan cooking, and you have a winner. Like Barry Bonds, a fish on tofu can hit seventy-three home runs a year.

1 PLATTER, SERVES 2 | PREP TIME: 1 HOUR + OVERNIGHT | COOKING TIME: 20 MINUTES

INGREDIENTS

Advanced Preparation
¼ cup mushroom water (see page 70)

For the Sichuan Sauce
1 tablespoon vegetable oil
1 tablespoon minced garlic
½ tablespoon minced fresh chilies (Thai chili or jalapeño)
½ cup hoisin sauce
1 tablespoon sweet soy sauce
¼ cup thin soy sauce
1 tablespoon fermented black beans,* washed, patted dry, and crushed
2 tablespoons Chinese sugar
1 tablespoon sherry cooking wine
2 tablespoons Shaoxing wine*
1 tablespoon Chinese red vinegar*
2 tablespoons white vinegar
1 tablespoon Chinkiang vinegar
1 tablespoon sesame oil
½ tablespoon Sichuan peppercorns, ground
¾ cup slurry (see page 69)

For the Mapo Tofu
2 tablespoons vegetable oil
1 tablespoon minced garlic

1 tablespoon minced ginger
½ tablespoon dried chili pepper, minced
1 tablespoon Sichuan peppercorns, freshly ground
3 tablespoons ground pork
1 tablespoon chili-garlic paste
3 tablespoons Sichuan sauce*
½ tablespoon fermented black beans,* washed, patted dry, and slightly crushed
2 tablespoons thin soy sauce
3 tablespoons Shaoxing wine*
1 tablespoon sesame oil
1 tablespoon MSG
2 cup large-dice firm tofu

To Prepare
1½ pound striped bass, red snapper, or bronzini; cleaned, scaled, deboned, and filleted (you can request the fishmonger do this)
¼ cup vegetable oil
½ cup cornstarch
3 tablespoons sweet chili sauce (Mae Ploy is a good brand)
1 finger ginger, julienned
1 scallion, sliced

(Continued on next page)

COOKING PROCEDURE

Advanced Preparation
First, make your mushroom water (see page 70) and let it rest in the refrigerator overnight.

For the Sichuan Sauce
Place a sauce pot on medium heat and add the vegetable oil. Once the oil is hot, add the garlic and fresh chilies, and cook through, 2 to 3 minutes.

Add hoisin sauce, soy sauces, bean paste, sugar, and the sherry and Shaoxing wines; bring to a boil. Next, incorporate all the vinegars, the sesame oil, and the peppercorns.

Bring back to a boil and add slurry to thicken the sauce. Reserve.

For the Mapo Tofu
Heat wok or pan on medium heat and add vegetable oil.

Add the garlic, ginger, dried chili, and peppercorns, and cook through for 3 minutes.

Turn heat to high, add ground pork, brown, and flip to brown the other side.

Next add the chili-garlic paste, Sichuan sauce, dried chili, and black beans. Cook for 3 minutes. Then add the thin soy sauce, mushroom water, Shaoxing wine, sesame oil, MSG, and tofu.

Simmer it for 5 minutes until it reduces.

For the Crispy Fish
Cut your fish into six slices and pat dry. Heat a pan on high and add ¼ cup vegetable oil to pan.

Dredge the fish in cornstarch.

Add the fish to the pan, skin-side down, searing until crisp. Flip and do the same to the other side until cooked through. Cooking times will vary based on the fish.

Remove fish from the pan and reserve.

Finishing Touches
Transfer everything in the pot with the tofu to a serving bowl. Top the tofu with the fish.

Drizzle the sweet chili sauce over the fish and garnish the plate with ginger and scallion.

Pour some baijiu and get into a Sichuan peppercorn–eating haze.

> Tip:
> For this recipe, you can have the fish filleted and bones removed by the fishmonger. Crispy fish is usually served whole and makes for a dramatic presentation, but since it is sitting on a bed of tofu, it's a lot easier to eat sliced from a fillet.

CHAPTER 8

MEAT AND POULTRY

As much as Chinese food revolves around seafood, there is one thing you can count on when it comes to Chinatown: the ducks hanging in the restaurant windows. They have been watching us.

From the first batch roasted up in the morning on Eighth Avenue in Brooklyn to the stragglers hanging well past midnight at Great New York Noodletown, these fatty delicious gargoyles have been seeing Chinatown live, work, and eat since its inception.

They witnessed the tragedy of September 11, the magic of "Linsanity," and generations of Chinese families realizing the American dream. They still hang there to this day, steady and true and symbols of Chinese culture, community, and cuisine.

Those ducks have also seen some great restaurants close their doors forever, leaving only the memories of iconic Chinatown meals: the pork chops and rice rolls at South Wind; beef with peas at Joy Luck; and even the pastrami on rice at Ging Sun. These restaurants (and so many more) were all well-known in the Chinatown I grew up in, and were major players in defining a

cuisine and the community for the last half a century.

The owners and chefs of these places immigrated from China, just like my grandparents did. They opened their establishments and worked those woks for their whole lives. The money they earned sent their kids to college and made doctors and accountants out of them.

Recently, many of those old folks knew it was their time to sit in the sun and walk away from a life of hard work. Their sons and daughters, most of which had already had chosen their own path, with careers and kids of their own, would not return to keep these restaurants going. There ain't nothing better than the American dream, but I do miss the food I can never get again.

To Yuen Yuen, Silver Palace, Shin Kee, Hey Hey, Ging Sun, Wong Kee, Mon Bo, Joy Luck, South Wind, and all the rest: May you all know that the hard work to make your noble food was remembered and greatly appreciated. The dishes and the people that made, served, and cleaned them are a part of Chinatown forever. Your contribution to the community makes us all appreciate that Chinatown still stands. That it still is a neighborhood of hardworking people that make and eat great food, and that things also matter in Chinatown. I feel happy knowing after all these years, our community's kids are still eating and loving some of the same great dishes I ate as a kid and will grow up having an even better chance of success in this world.

Orders

Chinese food for those of us who grew up, live, and work here is not Sunday dinner at the local Chinese restaurant, slurping egg drop soup and crunching on egg rolls (that's reserved for an occasional Saturday night, after the club). We are busy workers that get hungry and want satisfying, affordable food in our daily lives to keep us going.

We call them "orders." My coworker will turn to me and ask "We getting orders for lunch?" Basically, they are simply-made meats served over rice. Many cultures around the world have some version of this. Sometimes they include vegetables, seafood, or noodles, but most often it's meat on rice.

Walk around the neighborhood during the day and you will see locals sitting outside, often in the park, faces buried halfway into a single white takeout container, scooping rice into their hungry mouths. Hell, some people just squat down and start chowing down right on the corner stoop. One-plate meals over rice are the preferred choice for those who live and work in Chinatown, as opposed to the multiple varying courses often associated with the cuisine.

Each restaurant usually has its own specialty when it comes to orders: velveted beef stir-fried and mixed with a loose egg, oyster sauce, and rice; fried pork chops with chilies and garlic over rice; the iconic BBQed duck over rice. All of the best are within walking distance of one another and worth the trip, depending on what you are craving that afternoon. (We don't use Yelp; we just know.) Many of these establishments have been there since I was born.

This is the food that fuels Chinatown. It makes us happy enough to finish the workday, already thinking about what order we will have for dinner, if nobody is cooking at home.

BBQED ROAST DUCK

Although many of the same cooking techniques are used, BBQed roast duck and the famous Peking duck are not the same. Peking duck is sublime, more expensive, and the service of this dish is extremely precise from the kitchen to the table to your plate. It's roasted to order, given a hot oil bath, fully taken off the bone, and served with its crispy skin as the star. It's a delicate, special-occasion dish.

BBQed roasted duck is served at room temperature, on the bone, with all the meat and a crisp skin that will slightly diminish as it hangs waiting for a hungry diner. It's our go-to food that makes us happy to eat in our daily lives, and is just as much a masterpiece as the Peking version.

Be ready to have some self-control and to not eat this hot, no matter how magnificent it looks like coming out of the oven. It's not resting, it's bringing it down to room temperature, which is important for Chinese BBQ (and BBQ in general). This process allows the fat, juices, and meat to be at optimal eating conditions. Just know that when you get this right it's like hitting the DK Milly Maker.

Disclaimer:

This is not an easy dish to prepare. You need a lot of time, and a lot of room. I've made it my mission to make this an easier dish to master, so that hopefully in a couple of tries you will be able to snatch that pebble from my hand.

---

1 PLATTER, SERVES 4 PEOPLE | PREP TIME: 1 HOUR + DRYING TIME FOR THE BIRD | COOKING TIME: 1½ HOURS

INGREDIENTS/EQUIPMENT
1 Long Island Peking Duck, whole, head on
1 set of BBQ hooks

For the Chinese Five-Spice Rub
2 tablespoons kosher salt
2 tablespoons Chinese five-spice powder
4 tablespoons sugar

For the Hoisin Mix
3 tablespoons hoisin
2 tablespoons ground bean sauce (Koon Chun)*
1 piece star anise

For the Maltose Mix
7 tablespoons maltose
3 tablespoons white vinegar

For the Sauce
¼ cup duck jus, from duck water in the roasting pan, strained
1 tablespoons thin soy sauce
2 tablespoons hoisin mix (see above)

(Continued on page 123)

★ Can be purchased online or at most Chinese supermarkets.

COOKING PROCEDURE

Clean the cavity of the duck, removing all organs, then rinse it clean. If there is no cavity, cut a 3-inch slit in the middle of duck, just below the breastbone.

Combine the all of the five-spice powder rub ingredients and mix. Rub the five-spice rub all over the inside and outside of the duck. Then, rub 2 tablespoons of the hoisin mix inside the cavity wall. Seal the cavity with a wooden or metal skewer. Pierce the skin and bring the tip of the barb through the skin on the other side of the cavity and work your way up until it's stitched. If you are working with a duck without a head, seal the top opening of the duck as well.

Attach each BBQ hook under the wing's "armpits" in the back and put the head through the ring (if no head on the duck, the ring will just remain empty).

Combine the ingredients for the maltose mix in a sauce pot. Warm slightly to liquefy and mix both ingredients.

Fill a large stockpot ⅔ of the way up with water and bring to a boil. Dip the duck into the pot for 1 minute and make sure the duck is submerged in the water, holding it by the hooks, then remove. Pat dry completely.

Brush the maltose mixture all over the duck and hang over a catch pan. You can use a fan to speed the process up of drying the duck skin. Hang until the skin is smooth and dry. Drying times vary and general food-handling regulations allot no more than 2 hours to leave cooked meat out at room temperature. You better set your fan on high.

Set up a roasting rack with a hotel pan under it in a 360°F oven. Once positioned, pour water into the pan, filling to ½ inch up the sides. Remove the hooks and lay the duck, breast-side up, on the rack. Make sure the duck is exactly in the middle of the rack. Fold back the head and wings so the duck is raised up at a 20-degree angle (so it basically sits on a pillow of its head and wings). This allows for better airflow—in a restaurant we would actually cook it in a big oven while it hangs from the hooks, but home ovens typically aren't big enough to cook it that way.

It is done when golden brown, has a crispy skin, and the internal temperature reaches 175°F (for some, anything past 165°F is overcooking, but in my experience the duck has a lot of fat that at 165°F leaves some areas a little rare, and that is not best for this style of eating duck). Turn off the oven and let the duck rest about 20 minutes. Reattach the hooks to the backs of the wings "armpit" and hang until it reaches room temperature, about 45 minutes.

Remove the skewer from the duck over a container and release the liquid from inside the duck's cavity. You can strain this liquid and add to your sauce, but it tends to be a bit too gamey, so do so with restraint.

Remove the hooks and lay on a cutting board, breast-side up, and cut off the duck's head and neck with your cleaver (Merry Christmas, Ralphie), then cut through the breastbone then cut down the backbone. Separate the breast, the legs, thighs, and the back. Hack those down to bite-sized pieces.

Mix the sauce ingredients together in a bowl. Transfer duck to a platter, and serve with the sauce and jasmine rice.

VELVETED BEEF WITH PEAS

Pork is the meat used most often in Chinese cooking, but many recipes have been adapted to the tastes of Chinese people in America, where beef is much more accessible and cheaper than it is in China. There is a whole genre of velvet beef dishes served over rice that Chinese people order all the time: beef with egg, beef with tomatoes, beef with peppers and black beans, and this one, beef with peas.

These dishes are different from those famously modified for the American palate like General Tso's Chicken or egg rolls, and offer a glimpse into a lesser-known niche in Chinese cooking: specifically, Chinese food reimagined for Chinese people living in Chinatown. They are never publicized, and none are famous, so they remain under the radar and are Chinatown's best-kept secret.

1 PLATTER, SERVES 2 | PREP TIME: 20 MINUTES + OVERNIGHT | COOKING TIME: 6–8 MINUTES

INGREDIENTS

1 cup velvet marinade (see page 70)

6-ounce flank steak, sliced on the bias

¼ cup mushroom water (see page 70)

3 tablespoons vegetable oil

2 tablespoons diced white onion

1 tablespoon minced garlic

½ tablespoon minced ginger

½ cup peas, blanched and shocked, if fresh

½ cup oyster sauce

¼ cup thin soy sauce

¼ cup Shaoxing wine*

½ tablespoon MSG

2 tablespoons slurry (see page 69)

1 egg, beaten

Jasmine rice, for serving

COOKING PROCEDURE

Marinate sliced beef in velvet marinade, cover, and let it sit overnight in the refrigerator. Separately, prepare your mushroom water and let it rest in the refrigerator overnight. (See page 70 for velveting and mushroom water ingredients and instructions.)

The next day, heat your wok or pan to medium heat and add vegetable oil.

Once the pan is hot, add the onion, garlic, and ginger, and cook through for 2 minutes.

Separately, set your fry pot to 350°F. Check with an instant-read thermometer. When it reaches 350°F, flash-fry the beef for 5 seconds.

Turn up the heat in the pan with the garlic and add the beef, tossing and browning on both sides, about 1 minute per side.

Next, add the peas, oyster sauce, and soy sauce, and reduce slightly, letting it simmer in the pan for 1 to 2 minutes.

Then add the wine, mushroom water, and MSG, reducing on a simmer for 2 minutes. Add the slurry to thicken the sauce, then turn off the heat.

Pour the beaten egg over the top, mix it in slightly, and transfer to a platter. Serve with jasmine rice.

---

* Can be purchased online or at most Chinese supermarkets.

CHINESE SAUSAGE AND POTATOES

This is our version of meat and potatoes that has a comforting savory flavor, perfect served over a bowl of rice. Chinese sausages have a savory-sweet quality that is hard to describe in any way other than "damn good." The texture is similar to certain styles of European charcuterie like salami or chorizo, but is fatty enough to stand up to additional cooking. The sausage is made from sun-dried pork and comes in many different varieties, all of which can be found at the Chinese markets. This recipe represents everything classic about Toisan food in one single dish of boiled potatoes soaking in the essence of the Chinese sausage, which is brought home with a hit of soy sauce.

1 PLATE, SERVES 2 | PREP TIME: 15 MINUTES | COOKING TIME: 35 MINUTES

INGREDIENTS
2 Idaho potatoes, peeled and sliced into ¼-inch thick wedges
1 gallon cold water
¼ cup salt
1 cup chicken stock
¼ cup thin soy sauce
2 tablespoons oyster sauce
4 Chinese sausage, sliced into ¼-inch rounds

COOKING PROCEDURE
Place potatoes in a large pot with cold water and salt, and boil until they are almost done, approximately 25 minutes. Remove the potatoes from the water and set aside.

Heat a separate saucepan to medium heat and add the chicken stock, then the soy sauce and oyster sauce.

Next, add the potatoes and the Chinese sausage, then simmer for approximately 5 minutes. You will notice the broth thicken slightly.

Transfer to a plate. This dish is best served over jasmine rice.

CHAR SUI ROAST PORK

Chinatown BBQ shops are defined by the rows of beautifully hung meats displayed right in the front window, uneven wood cutting boards, the big cleavers and the chefs that command them. Classic Hong Kong BBQed meat, give me a plate of that and it's going to disappear fast. This is the best of the best.

The technique in BBQ is an art, and Hong Kong BBQ is no exception. The trial and error of developing a skill set to properly prepare, dry, and cook meat according to tenderness and fat content—while paying particular attention to cooking of the skins of poultry and pigs—is one that seems like an impossible task. Just the technique of cooking in the oven for even airflow and hanging to rest is genius (although watch those hooks, they hurt when they catch you not paying attention). In China, they even invented the first barbecue oven, which was made of clay and powered by bamboo. That is something special for a cuisine that doesn't use ovens for primary cooking.

If shumai and *har gow* are the stars of dim sum, roast duck and especially *char sui* roast pork are the megastars of Chinese BBQ. The cut of the pig is from the shoulder, across the butt (a butcher term that has nothing to do with a butt). It's marinated, hung, and slow roasted until it's tender and then blasted to form a caramelized outer crust that gives a hit of charred bitterness, which your mouth seems to long for without you even realizing it. It is served at room temperature, which is the best temperature to eat it. Leftovers will find their way to roast pork bao buns, noodles, and fried rice, but there is nothing like this meat as BBQ. It deserves first billing when done right.

1 PLATTER, SERVES 6 | PREP TIME: 5 HOURS + OVERNIGHT | COOKING TIME: 1–1½ HOURS

INGREDIENTS/EQUIPMENT
1 pound pork butt (ask the butcher in the Chinese supermarket to cut into char sui strips)
1 set of BBQ hooks

For the Brine
1 gallon water
1½ cup kosher salt
¾ cup sugar
2 pieces star anise

For the Marinade
6 tablespoons garlic
½ white onion, diced
2 cup hoisin sauce
½ cup ground bean paste*

½ cup dark soy sauce
½ cup oyster sauce
2 tablespoons sesame oil
¼ cup Shaoxing wine*
2 tablespoons Chinese five-spice powder
½ cup honey
1 cup maltose
½ tablespoon fermented black beans,* rinsed, patted dry, crushed
2 tablespoons MSG
½ cup slurry (see page 69)

For Basting
¼ cup maltose

(Continued on next page)

---

* Can be found online or at most Chinese supermarkets.

COOKING PROCEDURE

For the Brine
Combine brine ingredients together. Add in the pork strips; let them soak for 4 hours in the refrigerator.

For the Marinade
Combine marinade ingredients together in a sauce pot (except for the slurry).

Heat the marinade, bring to a boil, add the slurry, and thicken the marinade. Set aside 1 cup of marinade to use as the sauce.

Remove the pork from the brine and add to the marinade while marinade is hot. Let sit overnight in the refrigerator.

Cooking the Pork
Remove pork from marinade and pat dry. Put maltose in a saucepan and warm to loosen. Then baste the pork with maltose.

Heat oven to 325°F. Set up a hotel pan with a roasting rack over it. Then pour water into hotel pan to ½ inch up the pan.

Lay the strips on the roasting rack and cover with aluminum foil and roast until the internal temperature is 180°F. Baste with maltose, then turn oven up to 450°F and remove the foil.

When the internal temperature is 210°F, turn off oven and let rest for 10 minutes. Then attach to the hooks to ends of the strips and let hang under a catch pan for 30 minutes or until it reaches room temperature.

Strain the pan drippings from the hanging pork, add to reserved marinade, and mix well to create the sauce.

Remove the char sui pork from hooks and place on a cutting board. Cut ¼-inch thick slices and transfer to a platter.

Transfer to a plate. This dish is best served over jasmine rice.

Tip:
Do not cut this thin when serving. It needs a meaty bite and the thinner you cut BBQ the drier it tends to be. There is also a fatty and a lean side to the meat, much like brisket in American BBQ, so expect that as you serve it. The fatty side tastes better, but may have a heavier chew depending on the pig. Don't slice with your cleaver; bring it down with force and use the weight of the cleaver to cut separate quarter-inch slices. Just watch your other hand. You don't want to mistakenly hack it off—it won't taste nearly as good.

SOY SAUCE CHICKEN

I remember Yuen Yuen, which is now closed. It was a favorite Chinatown restaurant on Bayard Street. The place had a front window that opened up where the lady who everyone in the community knew served fresh-squeezed orange juice from her trusty juicer for thirty years (maybe more). I had lunch there at least once a week for years. Their plate of three treasures rice consisted of soy sauce chicken, Chinese sausage, and a fried egg.

A slight tear forms in my eye whenever I think about this place, like it does whenever my favorite restaurants close their doors forever. You have to take a deep breath and realize there is not much you can do but hang your head in despair, and accept that there is one more precious thing taken from this world. (That, and do your best to recreate their dish and include it in your first book so their legacy lives on in its pages.) I thank them for all their years of hard work and for their famous soy sauce chicken, which is one of the best things I remember eating in all my life.

1 PLATTER, SERVES 6 | PREP TIME: 1 HOUR | COOKING TIME: 3 HOURS + 1 HOUR FOR THE BIRD TO REST

INGREDIENTS/EQUIPMENT

For the Chicken
1 whole (3½-pound) chicken
1 set of BBQ hooks

For the Broth
6 quarts chicken stock
4 pieces star anise
2 tablespoons cumin seed
½ tablespoon ground cloves
1 stick cinnamon
2 fingers ginger, peeled
1 tablespoon ground nutmeg
4 dried orange peels
½ cup kosher salt
2 cups Chinese sugar
2 cups thin soy sauce
½ cup double black soy sauce

For the Ginger Scallion Sauce
½ cup ginger, finely minced
1 cup minced scallion
1 teaspoon MSG
1 pinch sugar
½ tablespoon salt
1 chip star anise (break off a piece from 1 star anise)
½ cup vegetable oil
1 tablespoon sesame oil

> Tip:
>
> Many Chinese dishes source freshly killed chicken versus commercially raised birds that are processed for many days before reaching your cutting board. There is a big difference in the taste and texture of the meat, and worth a try cooking, if you can get them.

(Continued on page 133)

COOKING PROCEDURE

For the Chicken

Clean the cavity of the chicken and rinse.

Soak chicken in warm water for 30 minutes. Remove and attach barbecue hooks through the back into the wings.

Fill a stockpot with all the broth ingredients; simmer on low heat for 2 hours. Submerge the chicken into the stock and bring back to a simmer; continue to simmer for 15 minutes. Make sure you rest the hooks on the rim of the pot so you don't have to fish them out of the hot broth.

Turn off fire and pick the chicken up with the hooks. (Be careful! They'll be hot!) Dunk the chicken back into the stock, making sure the stock has entered the chicken's cavity.

Bring stock back to a simmer, turn off the fire, and let the chicken sit in the stock for 20 minutes. (Confirm the temperature of the chicken with an instant-read thermometer at 165°F. If you need more cooking, return the stock to a simmer and finish the cook.)

Remove the chicken from the pot and hang it to dry over a catch container.

When it's cooled to room temperature, remove the hooks, break it down on a cutting board, and transfer to a serving platter. Serve with the sauce.

For the Sauce

Place the ginger, scallion, MSG, sugar, salt, and star anise in a metal mixing bowl.

Place the vegetable and sesame oils in a saucepan and heat until you see a whiff of smoke.

Pour the oil into the ginger mix, let it cool down a bit, and remove the star anise.

Transfer to a serving bowl and serve with the chicken.

Tip:

Whole-chicken cookery is difficult, especially at restaurants. It takes more time to cook than most customers will wait for. The legs and thighs take longer to cook than the breasts, and the breasts tend to dry out quickly. The skin is thin and areas with little fat have no protection from the heat of cooking. Chinese BBQ solves a lot of these problems.

CHAPTER 9

DAMN GOOD SNACKS

Snacks are the best part of Chinese food and are essential to daily life. A typical day starts with waking up to a bowl of congee, then meeting friends for dim sum, and then shopping for scallion pancakes, bao buns, and other tasty treats. Break for noodles over a late lunch, and you have snacked all the way up to dinner.

Chinatowns across New York City are filled with countless options that are perfect for getting your snack on.

A stroll along the sidewalks of Flushing, Queens, is reminiscent of the markets in Shenjiamen, China. So many vendors and so many snacks, so little time. Walk slow, and venture down into the food courts that make up a lot of the interesting food finds in this Chinatown.

In these little hole-in-the-wall stalls, you will find a different variety of snacks that you may not find anywhere else in New York City. Sesame breads, offal skewers, and huge bowls of prepared seafood are hidden in a labyrinth of shops, which are fun to get lost in as you shop and eat.

In Brooklyn, Chinese families settled in immigrant-friendly neighborhoods after a boom of mom-and-pop businesses, and subsequently the Chinese markets opened their doors, along with noodle joints, BBQ eateries, bubble tea shops, and bakeries all along Eighth Avenue in Sunset Park and in Bensonhurst.

I watched them grow and expand and develop into a close-knit community of hardworking families who really know how to cook and eat great food, and support one another. Houses were bought, kids were sent to school, and new Chinatowns were born all through noodles and buns.

Like Queens and Brooklyn, Manhattan's Chinatown has its share of great places to satisfy your cravings of awesome snacks, too. However, this Chinatown has been around for over a hundred years.

Most of its hardworking locals originally acquired their tasty treats from those little coffee and teahouses, the ones that inspired my restaurant East Wind Snack Shop.

These old-school joints were cozy counters that hooked you up with all the classic snacks you could eat. When they were busy, you stood there in a mob like a Wall Street stock floor scene, where you would shout out your orders and you would get your box of goodies at some point, but you would also need a Quaalude to kill the stress of being there on a Sunday morning.

Despite most of those coffee and teahouses closing, so many specialty food places that make everything fresh and from scratch still exist and are open all day on Mott, Pell, and Bayard Streets, so have a blast as you go down the rabbit hole of snack varieties. Freshly pressed tofu, house-made sweet soy milk, Chinese sausages, and street vendors selling everything from fruit, *joong*, fresh rice noodles, hot cakes, and panfried breads are all available to you here.

Tour each Chinatown's streets and enjoy a taste of the snack culture of China, or try making some of my favorites right here with these recipes.

PORK BELLY BAO BUN (GUA BAO)

These became very popular over the years in NYC. The bun is a soft, white, puffy clamshell in which you serve various meats and vegetables. You will occasionally see this bread as the vehicle for eating Peking Duck and *char sui bao*.

You simply steam the buns back to their original swollen state. They will last in the steamer for a while like this, so if you want to keep them hot while cooking, just lower the heat on the steamer. However, they do lose quality the longer they sit out at room temperature, so plan to eat them quickly (which shouldn't be a problem).

MAKES 6 GUA BAO BUNS | PREP TIME: 2½ HOURS | COOKING TIME: 10 MINUTES

INGREDIENTS

For Braising the Pork Belly
8-ounce pork belly, skin off
2 tablespoons all-purpose flour
1 tablespoon vegetable oil
1 cup Shaoxing wine*
¼ cup thin soy sauce
¼ cup dark soy sauce
2 tablespoons oyster sauce
1 tablespoon Chinese sugar
1 finger ginger, peeled, whole
1 clove garlic, whole
1 dried chili pepper, whole
1 piece star anise
3 cups water

For the Sauce
½ cup braising liquid, reserved from cooking the pork
¾ cup hoisin sauce
3 tablespoons oyster sauce
1 tablespoon Hoy Fung chili-garlic sauce
4 tablespoons sugar
1 pinch MSG

For Assembling the Buns
1 tablespoon vegetable oil
6 bao buns*
1 cucumber, sliced
1 tablespoon fried garlic
1 scallion, sliced

(Continued on page 139)

---

* Can be purchased frozen online, at most Chinese supermarkets, or at select grocery stores.

COOKING PROCEDURE

Braising the Pork Belly

Dredge pork belly in flour. Heat your pan to high and add the vegetable oil. Sear the pork belly on both sides, about 2 minutes per side. Add Shaoxing wine.

Next, add the soy sauces, oyster sauce, sugar, ginger, garlic, spices, and water (the liquid should cover ¾ of the pork belly; if not, add more water).

Simmer until soft and tender (you can use your instant-read thermometer until it reads 210°F). Remove from the heat and let the pork rest in the liquid until it cools down to room temperature.

Reserve the pork belly. Do not pour out the liquid left in the pan. (You need it for the sauce.)

For the Sauce

Strain the liquid from the pork belly braise and reserve ½ cup.

Combine all the sauce ingredients and mix well.

Assembling the Buns

Set up your steamer to high. Remove the top level of the steamer.

Slice pork belly into 6 equal slices, and place in a shallow bowl with 1 cup of the braising liquid. Place in the middle tier of the steamer until hot, approximately 6 to 8 minutes.

Rub a little vegetable oil on the top level of the steamer and place the 6 bao buns inside. Add this level on top of the level with the pork belly.

Steam for 5 to 7 minutes until both pork belly and buns are hot. Remove from steamer.

Open buns, place a slice of pork belly in each one, top with a slice of cucumber, and dress with a tablespoon of sauce. Garnish with fried garlic and scallion.

Transfer to a platter and serve.

SCALLION PANCAKES

I love telling people that China invented pizza. It's a huge debate, but the legend of Marco Polo has him bringing back scallion pancakes to Italy and you know the rest.

As you stroll along through the Chinese markets, you will notice all kinds of flatbreads, some glittered with sesame seeds, and freshly seared ones just glistening through the plastic partitions, calling you to chew on their salty, pull-apart magic.

Scallion pancakes, sesame bread, and *shaobing* (sao bing) are all types of northern Chinese flatbreads. The recipe I'm sharing with you is the style found mostly in Shanghai that is slightly thicker. These pancakes are made one by one (as opposed to the bigger round "pies") and contain an abundant amount of scallions, salt, and fat.

1 PLATTER, SERVES 6 | PREP TIME: 3 HOURS (OR OVERNIGHT IF DESIRED), FOR RESTING THE DOUGH | COOKING TIME: 6 MINUTES

INGREDIENTS

For the Dough
½ pound all-purpose flour
½ tablespoon kosher salt
½ tablespoon white sugar
7 ounces water

For Preparing the Pancakes
¼ cup kosher salt
½ pound unsalted butter
¼ cup sesame oil
¼ cup lard (see tip on page 142)
1 tablespoon MSG

Finishing Touches
2 scallions, sliced thin
½ cup flour for dusting
¼ cup vegetable oil
1 cup sesame seeds
½ cup thin soy sauce or Damn Good Dipping Sauce (see page 39)

COOKING PROCEDURE

For the Dough
Prepare your mixer with a hook attachment and place all dry ingredients in the mixing bowl.

Simmer your water, then slowly add to the bowl. Set mixer on setting one and mix until there is no more flour at bottom of bowl and the dough is smooth, approximately 10 minutes.

Remove the dough from the mixing bowl and place in plastic wrap. Let dough rest for 3 hours or overnight in the refrigerator.

Preparing the Pancakes
Place the butter, sesame oil, lard, and MSG in a saucepan, and heat gently until they are melted and incorporated.

Unwrap your dough and use a rolling pin (a large rolling pin, not the dumpling rolling pin) to flatten it to a square sheet about ⅛-inch thick. Dust with some flour.

Use a pastry brush to coat the sheet of dough with the fat mix. Sprinkle salt and scallions generously over the sheet.

On the long side of the sheet, roll up the dough from one end to the other so it's in the shape of a log with a swirled center.

(Continued on next page)

Dust the table with flour. Cut the dough log into 1-inch pieces. Place the circles flat on the table and dust with more flour. Then, take your rolling pin and lightly flatten the dough into a circle 3 inches in diameter and ¼ inch thick.

Panfrying the Scallion Pancakes

Heat a wok or pan to medium heat and add the vegetable oil.

When the oil's hot, add the pancakes, preferably three at a time, depending on the size of your pan. Don't overcrowd. Flip them when golden brown.

When both sides are golden brown and fully cooked through, pour sesame seeds onto a plate with a 3-inch spread, and press both sides of the pancake into the sesame seeds.

Transfer to a platter and serve with the soy sauce or Damn Good Dipping Sauce on the side.

Tip:

For the lard, if you refrigerate the braising liquid from the pork belly bao buns (see page 139) overnight and skim off the white fat that will form on top, it will work perfectly for this recipe.

COLD SESAME NOODLES

I first fell in love eating these noodles at a small Shanghainese restaurant on Oliver Street in Chinatown. It was one of the few Shanghainese places in the neighborhood, and there was nothing better on a hot day than slurping up these sweet, chewy, sesame-flavored goodies. My friends and I always looked forward these noodles, an alternative treat to our Cantonese diets we grew up on. We were missing out on all the regional greatness of Chinese cuisine, the chilies and peppers of Sichuan, the noodle soups of Lan Zhou, the chicken rice of Hainan, but we made sure we appreciated the beauty of Shanghai cuisine. The different textures, the sweeter flavors—and the noodles were served cold! This was awesome Chinese food!

Shanghainese food was something else, and I knew it from those noodles. Of course I loved the Cantonese food I was brought up on, but this style was so new and cool and different than what I was used to. You would mix the thick sesame sauce with the slick noodles, folding in the scallions and sesame seeds, then serve a chopstick full onto all your friend's plates. The slick wavy noodles would hang off your chopsticks slathered in that sauce, and then you would stuff them into your face and slurp up all that sweet glaze, occasionally hitting a slice of scallion and a hint of minced garlic and all those flavors would explode at the same time. Cold Sesame Noodles are the gateway food to the incredible wonders of Shanghainese cuisine.

1 PLATTER, SERVES 6 | PREP TIME: 30 MINUTES | COOKING TIME: 10 MINUTES

INGREDIENTS

For the Sauce
2 cups tahini paste
1¼ cups white sugar
½ cup Chinkiang vinegar
1 tablespoon sesame oil
2 tablespoons thin soy sauce
½ tablespoon dry chilies, crushed well
1 teaspoon powdered cumin
2 tablespoons Shaoxing wine*(

For Preparing the Noodles
¼ cup vegetable oil
3 tablespoons salt

1 pound lo mein noodles*
1 gallon ice water
2 tablespoons peanut oil (vegetable oil is okay, too)

For the Garnishes
2 scallions, sliced
¼ knob ginger, peeled and julienned
½ tablespoon cilantro, minced
½ tablespoon dried chili peppers, crushed
¼ cup peanuts, crushed
½ cucumber, sliced
1 tablespoon sesame seeds
½ tablespoon sliced Thai chilies or jalapeño*
  (optional)

(Continued on page 145)

★ Can be purchased online or at most Chinese supermarkets.

COOKING PROCEDURE

For the Sauce

Combine all the sauce ingredients except the Shaoxing wine in a bowl and mix well. Add the Shaoxing wine to help smooth it out.

Preparing the Noodles

Turn on a pot of water for blanching on high heat. Boil water, then add the vegetable oil and the salt.

Add noodles; cook until al dente. Follow the instructions on the packages, as it may vary depending on the type of noodles.

Remove the noodles and submerge in ice water. Remove, strain, and toss with peanut oil and 1 cup of the sauce immediately.

Transfer to a platter; top with ½ cup of the sauce and all the garnishes. Serve.

CONGEE

Congee is a naturally thickened rice soup. It is a grandparents' specialty that's simple to make. Simmer rice in stock, then add things like pork, preserved eggs, scallions, ginger, and cilantro.

This rustic soup makes moms so happy because it's a nutritious, hearty meal that needs only humble things to make it good. It's the dish you want to eat when you are sick. If you tell five little old Chinese ladies you aren't feeling well today, by tomorrow you will be brought five containers of congee. It's their anti-sick potion. It's breakfast, lunch, a late night snack, or a whenever-you-are-hungry kind of food.

In Chinese culture, every household has its own adaptation of this famous soup. Sometimes there are even conflicting schools of thought under one roof. Big chunks of ginger or minced? Soy or no soy? Best to eat at breakfast, lunch, or dinner? It's one of those dishes that separates the family and then instantly brings them back together once it's served.

MAKES 6 BOWLS | PREP TIME: 30 MINUTES | COOKING TIME: 2 HOURS

INGREDIENTS

2 quarts chicken stock

3 cups cooked leftover rice

1 finger ginger, peeled and coarsely chopped

1 tablespoon salt, or to taste

2 tablespoons MSG

1 cup pork belly, trimmed of its fat and minced (you can even go bacon!)

2 hundred-year-old preserved eggs,* minced

½ cup sliced scallion

¼ cup cilantro, chopped

¼ cup soy sauce

COOKING PROCEDURE

Bring the chicken stock to a simmer and add rice, gently breaking the kernels as you add them.

Simmer covered until the rice thickens the broth, stirring occasionally. This is a slow process that typically takes up to 2 hours.

Next, add coarsely chopped ginger and season with salt and MSG. Then add the pork belly to the pot and simmer until done, about 10 minutes.

Drop in the minced preserved eggs and simmer until they're hot, about 3 minutes.

Ladle the congee from the pot into bowls and top with scallion and cilantro. Serve with soy sauce on the side. Grab a spoon.

★ Can be purchased online or at most Chinese supermarkets.

SPRING ROLLS

As you may know, many Chinese families make dumplings on special occasions. My wife's family is originally from Shenjiamen, which is famous for dumplings. Because life is funny, on special occasions, they make spring rolls instead!

The family prepares the filling all night and then they roll all day. The moment we arrive at the house, they start frying. In minutes, all you hear is *crunch, crunch, crunch*. While most never enjoy spring rolls outside of a restaurant setting, they are special to my family as a home snack.

Spring rolls got their name because they are a traditional Spring Festival dish in China. "Crispy fat-bathed cylinders of awesomeness" is what they should have called them. Birthdays, Chinese New Year, even Thanksgiving and Christmas, we snack all day on these before we eat dinner.

Tips for Making a Great Spring Roll:

- First and foremost: Choose a good wrapper. There are a few good brands, including TYJ and Wei Chuan. Spring roll and egg roll wraps are best bought. The consistency and the way the wrapper absorbs oil and crisps are important and these brands provide both. They come in different sizes depending on how large you want your spring roll to be and how much filling you want it to have.
- When you remove the sheets from the package, your impulse will be to pull each sheet one by one to separate them, but it's much easier to separate half the sheets from one another, then half from that, and so on.
- Always roll them at the same size for consistency of cooking, which means portioning your filling.
- Roll each roll tightly to squeeze out any air, or the roll could collapse or explode in the frying process.

(Continued on next page)

SPRING ROLLS (CONTINUED)

MAKES 6 ROLLS | PREP TIME: 1½ HOURS + OVERNIGHT | COOKING TIME: 10 MINUTES

INGREDIENTS

For the Filling
½ cup mushroom water (see page 70)

¼ cup vegetable oil

1 tablespoon chopped garlic

1 tablespoon peeled and minced ginger

1 white onion, peeled and thinly sliced

3 cups red cabbage, thinly sliced

3 cups napa cabbage, thinly sliced

1 carrot, peeled and julienned

12 dried mushrooms, thinly sliced (from the mushroom water)

2 cups Shaoxing wine*

1 cup thin soy sauce

½ cup oyster sauce

2 cups bean sprouts

For Assembling the Rolls
¼ cup all-purpose flour

5 tablespoons water

6 sheets 8-inch spring roll wrappers

½ cup chicken thigh, deboned, skinned, and chopped

½ cup chopped raw shrimp, shelled and deveined

1 cup Damn Good Dipping Sauce (see page 39)

PREPARING THE FILLING

First, prepare your mushroom water (see page 70) and let it rest in the refrigerator overnight.

In a large skillet or wok, add vegetable oil and turn to medium heat. Next, add the garlic, ginger, and onion, sweat for 2 minutes or until soft, and turn heat to high. Then add the cabbages, carrot, and mushrooms, and cook for 3 to 4 minutes. Incorporate Shaoxing wine, soy sauce, oyster sauce, and mushroom water.

Remove from and place the mixture in a colander (or perforated hotel pan with a hotel pan underneath) with a bowl under the colander to catch the drippings. Top with plastic wrap, then place a weight (like a heavy can) on top of the mixture to drain the excess liquid, and refrigerate overnight.

Before rolling, add bean sprouts and mix.

ASSEMBLING AND COOKING THE ROLLS

Mix the flour and water to a paste. Separate 6 spring roll sheets.

Place each sheet on your work surface with the points on a diagonal like a diamond, then add ½ cup of filling just under the halfway point of each sheet.

Next, top 1 tablespoon of chicken and 1 tablespoon of shrimp onto the filling. Fold over the left point slightly, then the right point slightly. Roll the bottom point over the filling tightly and seal the edges with the flour paste.

Set your fry pot to 325°F. When the oil is hot, deep-fry the rolls; use your spider to weigh them down in the oil for 5 to 6 minutes. Stir occasionally for even cooking.

Shake out any excess oil, transfer to a platter, and serve with the Damn Good Dipping Sauce. *Crunch.*

★ Can be purchased online or at most Chinese supermarkets.

Tip:

Making *joong* is all in the preparation. Once that is accomplished, just steam or boil and eat. There are different wraps including lotus leaf, banana leaf, and bamboo leaf. The wraps are not for eating, but impart their fragrance when cooking, sending out a delicious aroma that catches you as you peel back the wrap to expose the sticky orbs of rice goodness. There are simple folds and elaborate ones. During events like the Dragon Boat Festival, the folds can get pretty intense.

JOONG

Joong (or *Zongzi*) is sticky rice mixed with meat and cooked from scratch so that the flavor of the meat melds with the sweet rice and is held together by a fragrant leaf wrap. You soak the rice in cold water overnight, and it will slowly absorb the water as it sits, like time-delayed osmosis, returning the kernels to their original state before they were dried and harvested. Then, just boil this perfect package.

You can mix and match accessories for the sticky rice. These wraps of Khan can be filled with dried shrimp, Chinese sausage, Chinese bacon, dried scallops, dried mushrooms, and preserved eggs. All that dried protein reconstitutes with the rice during the cooking process, yielding something more than the sum of its parts—and it may allow you to live long and prosper.

MAKES 6 *JOONG* | PREP TIME: 30 MINUTES + OVERNIGHT | COOKING TIME: 1 HOUR

INGREDIENTS
12 bamboo leaves* (see note below)

3 cups sticky rice, soaked in cold water overnight

½ cup Chinese sausage (*lap cheong*)*, sliced into rounds

½ cup sliced Chinese bacon (*lap yuk*)*

¼ cup dried shrimp*

¼ cup sliced dried mushrooms*

¼ cup slightly chopped dried scallop*

6 salted egg yolks*

1 tablespoon salted fish,* minced and bones removed (optional)

¼ cup raw peanuts, chopped

¼ cup mushroom soy sauce

Note:
There are both dry versions of bamboo leaves that need to be soaked in water overnight, and fresh/frozen iterations that need no preparation whatsoever.

COOKING PROCEDURE
If you are using dry bamboo leaves, remove them from the water.

Next, strain the sticky rice in a colander, and then transfer into a mixing bowl. Add the rest of the ingredients and mix well.

Fold up the *joong* mixture in the bamboo leaves: Roll 2 bamboo leaves into a cone shape and add approximately 1 cup (or ⅙) of the *joong* mixture. Fold the open end down to close the opening to form a triangle shape and tie with kitchen string.

If you aren't sure if you folded the leaves tight enough, it may be better to steam your joong so you won't lose your rice to the boiling water.

Fill a pot deep enough to hold your *joong* ⅔ of the way with cold water.

Place your *joong* into the water, weigh down with a plate, cover, and boil. (You can also place them in your steamer on high—either cooking method works equally fine.)

After 45 minutes to an hour, remove your *joong* and transfer to a serving platter.

---

* Can be purchased online or at most Chinese supermarkets.

TEA EGGS

Chinese New Year. We party on this holiday. It revolves around taking care of all things you need to wrap up from the previous year and preparing what you need for the coming year. It also recently became a school holiday in New York City, so having your kids around all day to celebrate makes for happy families and lots of red envelopes filled with money to celebrate the future fortunes of the children. It's the only day of the year I know that Chinese people want to take off from work to celebrate. Christmas, birthdays, even giving birth, Chinese people won't miss a day's work. That's just how it is, but on Chinese New Year businesses will close, parents will take time off, and families and friends will all get together and eat.

Tea eggs are symbolic of health and prosperity, and are made for several festivals and Chinese New Year celebrations. In a restaurant kitchen, they will lightly crack the shells of the eggs to allow the tea to stain the egg white and make a nice abstract design. Put them on rice or in noodle soup, or just eat them as a snack on their own.

MAKES 6 PORTIONS | PREP TIME: 5 MINUTES | COOKING TIME: 20 MINUTES + OVERNIGHT

INGREDIENTS
1 quart cold water
6 eggs
½ cup dark soy sauce
2 tablespoons black tea
1 finger ginger
1 tablespoon chili paste
1 tablespoon salt
1 piece star anise
1 teaspoon Chinese five-spice powder
¼ cup black soy sauce
Orange zest, from ½ orange

COOKING PROCEDURE
Pour cold water in a saucepan. In the pan, organize the eggs in a single layer.

Bring to a boil and cook for 2 minutes. Remove the eggs and shock them in ice water to stop the cooking.

Remove from water and crack shell lightly with the back of a spoon.

In the water that was cooking the egg, add the rest of the ingredients. Boil the mixture and reduce until there is ¾ left of it left in the pot.

Once the mixture has reduced, add the eggs and cook for 1 to 2 minutes, then remove from fire, let it cool slightly, cover, and place in the refrigerator overnight, occasionally turning eggs in the liquid.

Remove shell and serve eggs on a platter.

CHAPTER 10

BIRTHDAY DINNER

Chinatown changes when the sun starts to set. The markets start to pack up and close for the night, as do all those little hole-in-the-wall shops, bakeries, and what's left of the remaining teahouses in the neighborhood.

Dim sum will be hard to get, as those big box restaurants turn into dinner spots for tourists and large groups looking to celebrate job promotions, anniversaries, and of course, birthdays.

Huge neon signs of glowing dragons and phoenixes will start to light Chinatown, calling you to come on in to eat and drink. The rapid pace of the day—with all its artisanal specialties and mom-and-pop joints that cater to one customer at a time—give way to another Chinatown, one that feeds differently under the moon and night sky.

When it gets dark, Chinatown loves to party. Many places are built big to accommodate weddings or large parties. They have huge dining rooms for friends and families to celebrate as the stress and weight of the workday dissipates, and the cooler night air brings big delicious platters of food, happiness, and, of course, some beer.

While we love our home-cooked dinners at the Toisan table—with its sharp balance of salt represented through bean pastes, preserved foods, and soy, simmering their way into light, bright vegetables, fresh fish, seafood, and simple cuts of meats that all come together over bowls of rice—we also love to go out on special occasions.

Banquet-style dining is all about celebrating. Many dishes ordered at the banquet table symbolize family, prosperity, fortune, longevity, and luck. Lavish menus are presented for big parties. Whole birds, lots of seafood platters, and dishes with expensive ingredients like sea cucumbers and abalone are a big part of this genre of Chinese high-end dining with a focus on technique, ingredients, and plating.

Large platters are served in courses to be shared. The food will keep coming in multiple courses throughout the night. You will sit at a large table with eleven of your friends and family, snatch a lobster tail from a large lazy Susan, and drink toasts to bring better fortune and a happier life.

You can even book a karaoke room to eat dinner, drink, and sing, because we got that in Chinatown! Best of all, you will always eat an epic meal, which makes for very happy birthdays. If you look up your birthday on the lunar calendar, you can have this type of dinner twice a year! Roasted chicken or duck. Whole flounder or sea bass. Lobster or crab. Choose what you like, or order it all. It comes on big plates, served family style.

ROASTED CHICKEN, SALT, LEMON, AND SHRIMP CHIPS

Roasted birds are always magnificent at any dinner table. For Chinese celebrations, a whole chicken is ordered and represents togetherness with the family. It's like Thanksgiving on your birthday, but with chicken instead of turkey.

A whole chicken can be complicated to cook with precision because parts of the bird cook at different rates, but this dish utilizes several techniques that make chicken cookery yield juicier, crispier results. It combines brining, BBQ, roasting, and frying. This recipe calls for a hot oil bath instead of frying, because frying a bird whole needs some serious precision and care, and a big area to fry. Like the roasted duck recipe in this book, get your roasting rack ready and break out the BBQ hooks.

1 PLATTER, SERVES 4 | PREP TIME: 2 HOURS + DRYING TIME FOR THE BIRD | COOKING TIME: 1 HOUR

INGREDIENTS AND SPECIAL EQUIPMENT

For the Brine
1½ cups kosher salt
¾ cup sugar
2 pieces star anise
1 gallon water

For the Chicken
1 whole 3-pound chicken, brined
2 gallons water
1 set of BBQ hooks
7 tablespoons maltose
3 tablespoons white vinegar
½ gallon vegetable oil

Accompaniments
½ cup salt
2 tablespoons Chinese five-spice powder
½ tablespoon MSG
½ lemon, sliced into wedges
1 bag of Chinese shrimp chips

COOKING PROCEDURE

Combine all the brine ingredients and mix in the water. Submerge the chicken in the water and brine for 4 hours.

You brine the chicken because it's going to receive a lot of cooking and this will act as a safety blanket for dryness. Then it's simmered to a specific undercooked temperature to transform the proteins so you can dry the skin. It's hung for skin-drying, then roasted and given a fry bath for crispiness before serving. These steps make for an epic chicken.

Bring 2 gallons of water (or enough to cover the chicken completely) to a simmer in a large wide pot or, preferably, a wok. Attach BBQ hooks to the back "armpit" wings of the chicken and submerge the chicken in the simmering water. Holding it with the hook ends, you can ladle the water over the breasts, and cook until the internal temperature reads 110°F on your instant-read meat thermometer.

> **Tip:**
> For the shrimp chips, fry these yourself or buy them by the bag at the store. You can also use Pringles, as they are used on this dish at many restaurants, believe it or not.

(Continued on page 159)

COOKING PROCEDURE *(CONTINUED)*

Remove the chicken and hang over a catch container, patting it dry.

Mix the maltose and white vinegar together in a saucepan and warm to loosen. Then brush the whole chicken with the maltose mix.

Hang the chicken, placing a catching pan underneath, using a fan to dry it until skin is dry, keeping food safety regulations in mind.

Set up a roasting rack with a hotel pan under it in a 400°F oven. Once positioned, pour water into the pan, filling to ½ inch up the sides. Remove the hooks and lay the chicken breast-side up on the rack. Make sure the chicken is completely in the middle of the rack.

Fold back the wings so the chicken is raised up at a 10- to 20-degree angle (basically so the chicken looks like it's sitting on a pillow of its wings). This allows for better airflow. In the restaurant we would actually cook it in a big oven while it hangs from the hooks, but for home cooking the ovens aren't big enough to cook it that way. Roast until its internal temperature reaches 165°F, then turn off the heat.

Heat vegetable oil to 350°F in a sauce pot. Remove chicken from the oven and rest for 20 minutes. Drain any excess liquid from the cavity. Place the chicken in your wok or a big rondeau skillet.

Ladle the oil very carefully over the chicken in the pot just until the skin crisps up. Transfer the chicken to a cutting board, remove the hooks, and cut up the leg, thigh, breast. Place on a platter.

Mix the salt, Chinese five-spice powder, and MSG together, and place in a serving bowl to go with the chicken. Serve with lemon wedges and top with chips.

SHANGHAI BRAISED BLACK BASS

The fish is a symbol of prosperity and luck. Maybe the luck came from actually catching the fish, for anyone who has ever been fishing.

Black bass is another fish that can be found live in the tanks of many Chinese markets. Its sweet, tender, slightly flaky flesh is much like Shanghai's yellow flower fish, which is so good in Shanghai, but rare in fresh form in my neighborhood. This is the preparation straight from the woks of Shenjiamen. Purchase a fresh fish and let the simplicity of cooking and the flavors of the region shine through.

You will be cooking the fish in a broth of Shaoxing wine, soy, ginger, Chinese sugar, and a touch of star anise. The fish is submerged in this liquid and covered. The spirit flavor of this fish seems to flow out of it into the broth, converts to steam, glides along the top of the lid, and back down into the fish again. This is truly how fish should be cooked.

1 PLATTER, SERVES 4 | PREP TIME: 15 MINUTES | COOKING TIME: 15 MINUTES

INGREDIENTS

¼ cup vegetable oil

1½ pounds black bass, whole, cleaned, scaled, gutted, scored (ask the fishmonger to prepare this properly for you)

1 cup Shaoxing wine*

½ cup thin soy sauce*

¼ cup dark soy sauce

½ cup chicken stock

2 tablespoons Chinese sugar

½ finger ginger

½ piece star anise

1 tablespoon MSG

1 scallion, sliced

1 finger ginger, peeled and julienned

1 sprig cilantro (pick the leaves)

COOKING PROCEDURE

Heat your wok or pan and set to high heat. Add the vegetable oil and heat for 1 minute.

Lay the fish in the pan or wok and let sear for 1 minute. Add Shaoxing wine, soy sauces, and chicken stock.

When it starts bubbling, add the Chinese sugar, half a finger of ginger, star anise, and MSG, then cover the pan. Cook for approximately 12 to 15 minutes.

Transfer from pan to a platter and ladle 1 cup of broth to platter. Garnish with scallion, ginger, and cilantro leaves. Serve.

---

* Can be purchased online or at most Chinese supermarkets.

LOBSTER CANTONESE

This is the birthday dish for seafood lovers and it's a sign of good fortune, so spend the money on quality seafood to celebrate the money that will inevitably come your way next year. When your family takes you out to the Chinese restaurant to celebrate your birthday, they typically order this for you. If they don't, they are either broke or they don't like you very much. Happy birthday!

1 PLATTER, SERVES 4 | PREP TIME: 30 MINUTES | COOKING TIME: 15 MINUTES

INGREDIENTS

1½ pounds lobster,
   preferably live
¼ cup vegetable oil
1 tablespoon minced garlic
1 tablespoon minced ginger
2 ounces ground pork
½ tablespoon fermented
   black beans,* washed and
   pat-dried
3 tablespoon oyster sauce
1 cup seafood stock
   (or chicken stock)
2 tablespoons soy sauce
1 tablespoon MSG
1 pinch white pepper
¼ cup slurry (see page 69)
3 egg whites, slightly beaten
1 scallion, sliced into rounds
1 finger ginger, peeled
   and julienned

COOKING PROCEDURE

If you bought a whole live lobster, cut off the head, then crack the claws and knuckles. Cut the tail in quarters. (Be sure to cut just prior to cooking, lobsters don't last long when they are dead.)

Heat your pan to medium and add the vegetable oil. Then add the garlic and ginger, cooking through for 2 minutes.

Turn up the heat to high and add the lobster; mix in the pan gently. Next, add the ground pork and mix to brown slightly on all sides.

When the pork is browned, incorporate your fermented black beans, oyster sauce, and stock. Cover pan and reduce slightly for approximately 3 minutes.

When it's reduced, add your soy sauce, MSG, and white pepper. Thicken with the slurry.

Turn the heat to low. Slowly pour in egg whites and swirl the pan. Transfer to a platter and garnish with scallion and ginger.

Tip:

This dish varies depending on where you are ordering it, and most of it has to do with the lobsters. In New York City, we always have lobsters from Maine or Canada, which are the best you can buy. On the West Coast, they have Pacific lobsters that have a big tail, but no claws. This can drastically vary the taste. Some restaurants will even serve this dish as a duo with the addition of Dungeness crabs.

---

* Can be purchased online or at most Chinese supermarkets.

ROAST PORK LO MEIN

You ever watch a TV show or a movie where they order Chinese takeout? When they open the white takeout container and plunge the chopsticks into the box they always seem to pull out lo mein noodles. It's because they are that good. No matter what the conversation, the character has to slurp up some egg noodles before making their point in the scene. Clemenza was stuffing his mouth while conspiring to shoot Sollozzo in *The Godfather*, and that last noodle at the corner of his mouth could not be refused.

Lo mein noodles are a great canvas. They go with everything: beef, pork, vegetables, you name it. It soaks up all the sauce and seasonings while remaining bouncy, slick, and very slurpy. I admit, though, I have taken lo mein for granted. It's never what we order first, or look forward to eating, but at some point in the meal I always find myself slurping up those noodles, blissfully unaware of everything else is going around me. Great noodles will do that to you.

They are also a big part of birthday celebrations. The noodles are symbolic of longevity: the longer the noodle, the longer your life. It is also a sign that dinner is almost over, as the noodles and fried rice are usually the last savory courses served.

1 PLATTER, SERVES 2 | PREP TIME: 30 MINUTES (ADD TIME TO COOK ROAST PORK, IF YOU ARE MAKING IT YOURSELF) | COOKING TIME: 10 MINUTES

INGREDIENTS
¼ cup vegetable oil
¼ white onion, sliced
1 tablespoon peeled and minced ginger
1 tablespoon minced garlic
⅓ pound lo mein noodles
¼ cup oyster sauce
2 tablespoons thin soy sauce
1 tablespoon dark soy sauce
¼ cup snow peas, cleaned and trimmed
¼ cup sliced king oyster mushrooms
½ cup roast pork, slightly chopped (make yourself from the recipe on page 129 in this book or you can also purchase from any Chinese BBQ restaurant)
½ tablespoon fermented black beans,* rinsed, patted dry, and crushed into a paste
3 tablespoons chicken stock
½ tablespoon MSG
2 tablespoons slurry (see page 69)
¼ cup sliced scallions

COOKING PROCEDURE
Turn your blanching pot on and turn to high heat. Separately, turn on a sauté pan or wok to medium heat and add the vegetable oil.

Add the onion, ginger, and garlic to the sauté pan and cook through for 2 minutes. At the same time, drop your noodles into the blanching water, cook them for 3 to 4 minutes, and scoop them up with a strainer.

Turn up the heat in the wok to high and then add the noodles to the pan; swirl around with some chopsticks or the corner of your wok spatula.

Add the oyster sauce to the pan and let it reduce into the noodles, then add the soy sauces, snow peas, mushrooms, roast pork, black bean paste, chicken stock, and MSG, and cook for 2 to 3 minutes.

Do that swirl again with your chopsticks or wok spatula, then add the slurry to thicken the sauce.

Transfer the noodles to a serving platter and garnish with sliced scallions.

★ Can be purchased online or at most Chinese supermarkets.

CHICKEN AND SALTED FISH FRIED RICE

Rice, as you may now know, is integral to life in Chinese culture and symbolizes luck. At banquet celebrations like birthdays, it is always served fried. Plain rice is not served, unless requested.

It's also made at home. "Oh man, I made too much rice for dinner tonight" is code for "Fried rice tomorrow night!" Leftover steamed rice can morph into an amazing dish that can highlight any meat or vegetable yet still give the rice the spotlight. Fried rice embraces whatever ingredient comes its way.

The beautiful thing with fried rice is that you get to save the environment by recycling leftover rice, but the price is a night of slow drying in your refrigerator. You will never get the texture of true fried rice without this step.

1 PLATTER, SERVES 4 | PREP TIME: 30 MINUTES + OVERNIGHT | COOKING TIME: 8–10 MINUTES

INGREDIENTS

3 cups jasmine rice

½ cup chicken thigh, chopped and velveted (see page 70)

¼ cup vegetable oil

½ cup diced white onion

1 tablespoon minced garlic

1 tablespoon minced ginger

¼ cup carrot, small dice

¼ cup fresh peas, in season or frozen

1 tablespoon chopped salted fish* (see note)

2 eggs, slightly beaten

1 tablespoon kosher salt

½ tablespoon white pepper

½ tablespoon MSG

1 tablespoon soy sauce

3 tablespoons sliced scallions

COOKING PROCEDURE

Let me preface this by saying cooking fried rice is simple. However, the technical details still have to be followed. Proper preparation of the rice is key. For this dish, it's especially important to have all your ingredients at the ready and easily accessible. Many things in fried rice have different cooking times, and your timing has to be coordinated or you could overcook, undercook, or burn the dish easily. For this reason, oil temperature is very important.

Begin by steaming your jasmine rice and then cover and let it dry in your refrigerator overnight.

Next, prepare your velvet marinade, submerge your chicken, and place covered in the refrigerator overnight. (See page 70 for velveting ingredients and technique.)

Note:

There are small bones in salted fish, so cutting the meat off the end of the belly to the tail will yield meat with no bones. Salted fish can have a tough texture out of the package; it's easier to cut if you can steam the fish for ten minutes to loosen it up. Don't pick on it too much!

(Continued on next page)

★ Can be purchased online or at most Chinese supermarkets.

Heat your wok, cast-iron pan, or Teflon pan to medium high heat and add vegetable oil. (Rice likes to stick.)

You have to start with oil at medium to high heat to sweat your aromatics. Add the onion, garlic, and ginger and cook through for 2 minutes.

Flash-fry (see page 71) your velveted chicken in a fry pot for 1 minute, then add to the pan or wok.

Add your carrots, peas, and salted fish. Mix it all together and cook for 3 minutes. Once the vegetables are mostly cooked, pour in the eggs and stir vigorously and quickly to get a nice scramble.

Add in the rice and work it around the pan to coat it all with the fat and flavor. Press down with a rice scoop or spatula to separate kernels, then stir.

Add the kosher salt, pepper, MSG, and soy sauce, and stir. (Salt is used to cut the amount of soy, which will add too much liquid content to the rice.)

Transfer to a plate, top with scallions, and serve.

Tip:
The best way to dry the rice is to scoop out any leftover rice into a shallow perforated pan, cover the top with plastic wrap, and poke holes into the wrap and dry in the refrigerator overnight. The next day, take the rice and separate the kernels from each other gently between the palms of your hands. Separation will take on a glaze from the oil around each kernel when tossing in the wok. You can tackle any additional rice clumps in the wok by pushing the clump down with the wok scoop gently, as you want to keep the kernels in one piece.

CHAPTER 11

SWEETS

When you think back and reminisce about simpler times, there is usually something sweet involved. You return to your six-year-old self, walking from the store, one hand holding your mother's hand and the other clutching an ice cream cone.

Kettle corn, cotton candy, birthday cakes, Valentine's Day chocolates, Halloween candy—flash back and these things are often found in our favorite fuzzy memories. After a nostalgic sigh, a small smile returns to your face. You can still taste them.

It was summer, and we were kids just out of high school, that sweet time in your life just before you worked at a real job. We lazily spent it hanging out at the park on Mulberry Street, playing basketball and softball, spending weeks of doing nothing but hanging out with friends and watching this little old Chinese lady—seemingly no different than the ones who might assault you at the Chinese supermarket—make Hong Kong egg cakes in her little Chinatown stall.

Mrs. Cecilia Tam was the reigning Egg Cake Queen of Chinatown. Hers was the original "Cronut" line, stretching nearly a whole block, from somewhere on Mulberry Street all the way up Mosco Street to the corner, where it peeked into Mott Street.

Every type of person came for Mrs. Tam's egg cakes—us kids who lived in Chinatown, tourists, police officers from the nearby Fifth Precinct, teachers from the school across the street—and everyone waited, forking over their dollar for that bag of happiness.

She would open that hot pan, pour in that eggy, sweet batter, and purposely let it drip over the sides of the pan. You would watch it cook and that edge would crisp so beautifully. When a whiff of the batter hit your nose, you suddenly warped into a world you never knew existed. She flipped the pan over, popped out the bubbly, bouncy cake, separated the orbs, and into a clear wax paper bag it went.

I think about her often—how she always had a line, how she was always behind the pace, and how that turned out great for her. That meant every cake was made to order. She never sold a hotcake that sat for more than a minute. Every cake I had from another vendor was made to sit and wait for me to come and buy it, and they were never like hers. You have to ask: Did she make the line or did the line make her? This one little detail in a cooking discipline, like making a simple treat on the street to order, is all it takes sometimes to leave you with a sweet memory that will last forever.

HONG KONG HOT CAKES (EGG CAKES)

Desserts in Chinese cooking, from the perspective of a Chinese kid growing up in New York, didn't match the over-the-top sweet treats of the American dessert menu. Brownies, ice cream, and anything chocolate pulled me in and refused to let go. Mrs. Tam's dessert changed my mind.

As I mentioned in the beginning of the book, Chinese desserts are just different. Much less sugar is used, bean pastes replace cream and chocolate, and chewy textures are prized. Some even walk the line between savory and sweet.

The simplicity of a freshly cooked sweet pancake can be the gateway dessert. I know how good these cakes can be at their peak. In a *New York Times* review written by Ligaya Mishan, she likened my hot cakes (what we call them at East Wind) to the ones made by Mrs. Tam back in the day. (Yes, we make them to order.)

MAKES 8 HOT CAKES | PREP TIME: 20 MINUTES | COOKING TIME: 7 MINUTES PER CAKE

INGREDIENTS
4 egg yolks (reserve the whites)
¾ cup sugar
1/3 cup butter, melted
¾ cup whole milk
1 teaspoon vanilla extract
1 teaspoon almond extract
1 cup all-purpose flour
½ tablespoon baking powder
1 pinch salt
6 egg whites, whipped to soft peaks
1 tablespoon vegetable oil
Powdered sugar, to dust

Note:
You will have to buy a Hong Kong egg cake maker, electric or cast-iron, whichever is the most convenient for you.

COOKING PROCEDURE

Preparing the Batter
When cooking this recipe, remember that the batter is at its peak for just the day. The longer it sits, the more it will start to separate and will yield a much less crispy and vibrant hot cake. If you wait too long, it will be a "not-so-hot" cake. As in most situations, fresh eggs and dairy make a difference.

Prepare your mixer for use and attach the whisk to the mixer. Place the egg yolks in the mixer bowl and add sugar, whisking on high. If you don't have a mixer, you can just use a handheld mixer or hand-whisk.

Slowly add the butter and whip until smooth, then incorporate the milk, vanilla, and the almond extract.

In a separate mixing bowl, combine the flour, baking powder, and salt. Fold this mixture into the egg mixture gently with a spatula, just until it is incorporated. At this point, the batter should be pretty thick.

Next, fold in the egg whites, which will loosen up the batter slightly.

Cooking the Hot Cakes
Heat pan on medium heat (or set the machine). When hot, brush oil on both sides of the pan.

Spoon in the batter, letting some of it overrun the holes. Close the top and place back on the heat. Heat until one side gets golden brown.

Flip (note: flipping is not needed if you are using an electric egg cake maker), then let other side cook for just a minute. Be patient and wait until the last second before opening the clamshell.

Transfer to a plate and serve. Dust with powdered sugar.

BUBBLE TEA

The Bubble Tea Sweet Army has invaded the world. Now everyone loves slurping up milk tea with oversized straws and chewing on those sweet balls of tapioca. Bubble tea shops have opened with their famous shaking machines doing their dance to the enjoyment of kids and adults all over the globe.

Most bubble tea drink programs revolve around a large selection of flavors with chilled milk tea and chewy balls of tapioca in a clear plastic cup topped with a plastic heat-sealed sheet that allows a machine to shake it mechanically to emulsify the ingredients. A bow is tied to the cup in the form of a big fat colorful straw to allow for optimal slurping. The bubble tea movement now involves a selection of fruits and toppings and all sorts of clever Instagrammable ways to make it even more popular than it already was. It has become a "thing," as they say, and the chewy bubbles, once thought of as strange, are now addictive and fun.

4 SERVINGS | PREP TIME: 5 MINUTES | COOKING TIME: 15 MINUTES

INGREDIENTS

2 quarts water + 1 gallon for tapioca bubbles
2 cups dried oolong tea leaves
1 pack instant black large tapioca bubbles
24 ice cubes
8 tablespoons simple syrup
4 tablespoons condensed milk

COOKING PROCEDURE

For the Tea and Tapioca

Boil 2 quarts of water; once it boils, turn off the heat. Add the tea and stir. Let steep for 15 minutes and strain. Chill.

Boil 1 gallon of water, add the tapioca bubbles, and cook for 5 minutes. Note: There are multiple varieties in the market, each with slightly different cooking times, so follow the package instructions.

Strain tapioca, run under cold water for 1 minute, and reserve in cold water.

Fill 4 glasses with ice. Put 2 tablespoon of tapioca bubbles, 2 tablespoons of simple syrup, and 1 tablespoon of condensed milk in each glass.

Fill each glass with tea and stir well. Serve each glass with a big straw.

SESAME COOKIES

I could eat these tasty short cookies all day. They are a great snack bursting with sesame flavor and are perfect for Chinese New Year celebrations. This recipe yields cookies that have the same effect all great cookies have: they just dissolve in your mouth and it makes you want another cookie fast. Old school milk is not the drink of choice with cookies for Chinese people. Pairing these with cold, sweet soy milk hits the spot.

MAKES 36 COOKIES | PREP TIME: 20 MINUTES | COOKING TIME: 25 MINUTES

INGREDIENTS
½ cup butter
¾ cup shortening
1 teaspoon sesame oil
½ cup brown sugar
½ cup powdered sugar
2 eggs (1 for batter; 1 for egg wash)
1 teaspoon almond extract
½ teaspoon baking soda
½ teaspoon baking powder
1 pinch salt
2 cups flour
1 tablespoon sugar
½ cup sesame seeds

COOKING PROCEDURE

For the Dough

Prepare your mixer with paddle attachment and set to medium. (If you don't have a mixer, add 3 hours and a workout to the recipe.)

Place butter, shortening, and sesame oil in mixer bowl. Start the mixer and slowly add the brown sugar, then the powdered sugar, mixing until all ingredients are well incorporated.

Next, add 1 egg and mix until incorporated. Then add the almond extract. In a separate bowl, mix baking soda, baking powder, salt, and flour. Set your mixer to low and add the flour mix and mix for 15 seconds until just incorporated.

Remove the batter from your mixer. Roll into logs, wrap in plastic wrap, and refrigerate overnight.

Heat your oven to 325°F.

Remove plastic wrap from the dough logs and cut into ½-inch portions. Roll dough portions into balls.

Mix 1 egg with 1 tablespoon of sugar to make your egg wash. Coat each ball of dough lightly with egg wash using a pastry brush and toss in sesame seeds.

Place balls of dough on a slightly oiled sheet pan and press each one slightly.

Bake for 15 minutes, remove from the oven, and let them rest for 10 minutes.

Transfer to a platter and serve with some sweet soy milk.

LYCHEE CUSTARD TART (*Dàn Tat*)

Dàn Tat is the most popular dessert in Chinatown. *Dàn* means *egg* in Chinese. The name is derived from the English egg custard tart. It is a dim sum dish, but it is also sold in the bakeries and teahouses. In Macao, they call them Portuguese egg tarts. It's simply an egg custard in a shell, although there are some differences in the ingredients and the dough that makes the shells. The Cantonese version uses custard powder, and the crust is shorter than the puff pastry shells used in the Macao version.

It's a simple and delicious treat that I've eaten all my life and always enjoy. I have added lychees to my recipe because blessed be the fruit. I also like to serve it with a little vanilla ice cream. It's not traditional at all, but it's ice cream, for cryin' out loud!

MAKES 4 TARTS | PREP TIME: 2 HOURS + OVERNIGHT (TO REST DOUGH) | COOKING TIME: 15–20 MINUTES

INGREDIENTS

For the Tart Dough
8 ounces all-purpose flour

4 ounces butter, cut into small pieces and kept cold

3 ounces shortening, cut into small pieces and kept cold

1 pinch salt

1 tablespoon sugar

3 ounces water

1 cup flour, for dusting

1 egg

1 tablespoon sugar

Custard
⅓ cup sugar

9 egg yolks

3 cup cream

12 lychees (canned or fresh)

Finishing Touches
2 tablespoons coconut flakes

4 scoops vanilla ice cream

COOKING PROCEDURE

For the Tart Dough
Pulse half the flour in a food processor with the butter and shortening. Then add the salt, sugar, water, and remaining flour and pulse three times.

Dust your work surface with flour and transfer dough. Work the dough slightly to make sure the fat is incorporated into the flour. Wrap in plastic wrap and rest in the refrigerator for 3 hours or overnight.

Once the dough has chilled, dust the work surface with flour. With a large rolling pin, flatten the dough into a smooth sheet a touch thicker than ⅛ of an inch.

Turn your sheet over and trace circles into the dough with a paring knife to match the size of your baking mold.

Mix egg and sugar together. Using a pastry brush, coat both sides of your dough circles with the sugary egg wash.

Baking the Tart Shell
Grease tart molds and place dough circles into mold. Pull the dough up slightly and crimp the edges around the edge of the molds.

Dock the dough: Lightly poke the tart shell with a fork to yield holes that will allow steam to escape when you bake. Return to refrigeration for 1 hour.

(Continued on next page)

Make the Custard

Heat your oven to 350°F.

Divide the sugar between the egg yolks and cream in two separate pots. Heat the cream up to a simmer, temper (pour very slowly in increments) into the egg mixture, then whisk well.

Bake tarts for 2 minutes. Fill the tart with custard only half of its depth. Bake for 3 more minutes.

Add 3 lychees per tart and fill with custard to almost the top of the crust. The lychees will stick out halfway. Bake until done, approximately 8 minutes.

Remove the tarts from oven and let cool to room temperature. When serving, garnish with toasted coconut flakes and serve with a scoop of vanilla ice cream.

CHAPTER 12

CHINESE FOOD FOR THOUGHT

When I think about what makes Chinese food so damn good, many things come to mind, most of which are at the very least mentioned in this book.

The cuisine itself has been around for thousands of years, being passed on from generation to generation, from old-school to visionary, from grandparents to grandsons and granddaughters. This is happening right now, and before our eyes our food is evolving; epic new dishes are being created for our eating pleasure.

The history of Chinese food is rooted in peasant cuisine and draws its magic from making great dishes from the humblest of ingredients, and it respects a balance of flavor and texture, hot and cold energies, and sustainability. It utilizes some of the oldest techniques for baking breads, BBQ, dumpling making, stir-frying, and preserving foods that add those savory layers of complexity that are so important to our cooking.

There are so many styles based on the various regions of China—from seafood cooking in Shanghai, the spicy tastes of Sichuan, to the revered cooking of Hong Kong. Chinese food is found all over the world, and has adapted based on accessibility of ingredients, regional tastes, and economic status, yet it despite its differences, it all still remains Chinese food. It's there for everyone, no matter how rich or poor, Western or Eastern, kosher or halal, meat lover or vegetarian, to stay or to go.

All these things are vital to Chinese cooking, but it's the people that make it damn good. The people who cook it, the people who serve it, and all the people who love eating it. Chinese food people, as I'll call us, want to eat what we love, sitting at a table and requesting signature dishes from our favorite waiters.

Throughout this book, I talk a lot about going out to eat, enjoying meals with family and friends, and many things that we all love to do. These joyful instances are in the book because they are normal everyday things that we happily take for granted.

The thing is, I wrote this book in the spring of 2020, when we all took a trip into another world where those things now are a risk to do and maybe at risk of ever returning the way they once were.

I hope Chinese cuisine can pick up where it left off. We had a Chinese food renaissance going on in full swing. So many different styles of cooking from so many regions were getting their turn in the sun to show how delicious they are. Great creative chefs were strutting their stuff, business was good, and Chinatowns were flourishing.

Now that there are so many broken pieces, it will truly be a crossroad for Chinese culture, its food, and its people moving forward. We will not be an unfortunate victim of the pandemic. We will have to stand up for Chinatown, Chinese culture, and Chinese everything.

Every Chinese chef will need to take more risks, work harder, and cook better. Our voices will need to be louder, and the food tastier. We will need to teach, mentor, learn, and adapt. We're gonna need to cook our asses off, put on our game face, and be ready for whatever comes next.

★ ★ ★

I also need to address all this violence against Asians. I know there is a lot of hate out there. It's been there for a very long time, but it's on a roll now. Every time someone makes fun of Asians, it swells even more. Every time some ignorant chef says they love the food but insults the people who originally made it, it swells even more. And now our grandmothers and grandfathers are getting punched in the face just because they are Asian.

I won't stand for this. This has to stop. We have to help ourselves. Our unified voice has to be loud. Hear us. Respect us. We ain't just food. We are Americans.

ACKNOWLEDGMENTS

I have had a blast cooking throughout the years and many of those happy moments wouldn't have been possible without the support, teachings, love, patience, and friendship of all the people that I would like to thank while I have this opportunity.

To Laura, you do everything for me, and you are my everything and deserve every bit of credit. I could not have done anything in my life without you.

Jeremy, my son, you my man, always. I couldn't be more proud of you.

To my mom, the best mom ever, you are the strongest person I know. I love all of you with all my heart.

Thanks to my Aunt Sandra and Uncle Sai, for all the food tips and taking care of me! You two and the rest of the family, Aunt Mabel, Aunt Sarah, Aunt Lily, Uncle Joe, Jim, Tom, the other Uncle Tom. And of course my grandparents, Gong Gong and Paw Paw, Nai Nai, I miss you all.

Thank you, Mr. Lam, Sammy, and Yuki from Nobu; my chefs; Ed Brown, Nobu, and Jean-Georges Vongerichten—I learned so much from you all, I know it's never enough.

All my former sous-chefs and cooks, you know it's always a team effort.

Thanks to all my Columbus Park Boyz— you will always be family.

Thank you, Pete Lee and Ernest at Hop Kee, and Anthony Schirripa for asking, "You want a job cooking?"

To my AFM chefs, you guys rock!

Thanks to Jesse McHugh, my editor, for giving me the opportunity to write this book; to Alan Battman, for the great pictures; to every food writer who has ever been excited about my cooking; and to every fan of Chinese food out there.

A big hug and thank-you to everyone in my East Wind Snack Shop family.

A special thanks to Laura's parents, especially her dad, Hung Mau Chang.

ABOUT THE AUTHOR

When Chef Chris Cheung roamed Chinatown as a kid, the streets were lit and alive all day until late at night, businesses booming with tourists and locals hanging out drinking, shopping, and, of course, eating at restaurants.

He has been in love with Chinatown's food since the first spoonful of congee was stuffed into his hungry waiting mouth as a toddler. Home cooking and eating out in Chinatown helped him find his calling as a cook and later as a chef.

Throughout his career, he has worked with world-renowned chefs, many with Michelin and *New York Times* stars, as well as with high-powered restaurant groups that were a part of the Asian food explosion. Jean-Georges Vongerichten, Nobu Matsuhisa, the Iron Chef Morimoto, all influenced his training as a cook.

Chris has been in the industry for decades. He is currently the chef and owner of East Wind Snack Shop, an award-winning Chinese restaurant with two locations in Brooklyn.

He has said that he will never learn enough to satisfy his soul's craving for Chinese food, but he will happily share what he has learned.

The dishes chosen for this book offer his perspective on their importance to Chinese food in America and were developed traditionally, many from old-school sources. These recipes have evolved in his hands as he makes his small and humble contribution to this extraordinary cuisine.

He spent time in China cooking the old-school way in a country village farm on bamboo-fueled woks, and was mentored by a dim sum master chef as he furthered his study of Chinese cuisine. He took pearls of wisdom in cooking from his mom, his Aunt Sandra and Uncle Sai, and his wife's father and mother, anywhere he could get them.

CONVERSION CHARTS

METRIC AND IMPERIAL CONVERSIONS

(These conversions are rounded for convenience)

Ingredient	Cups/Tablespoons/Teaspoons	Ounces	Grams/Milliliters
Cornstarch	1 tablespoon	0.3 ounce	8 grams
Flour, all–purpose	1 cup/1 tablespoon	4.5 ounces/0.3 ounce	125 grams/8 grams
Flour, whole wheat	1 cup	4 ounces	120 grams
Fruit, dried	1 cup	4 ounces	120 grams
Fruits or veggies, chopped	1 cup	5 to 7 ounces	145 to 200 grams
Fruits or veggies, pureed	1 cup	8.5 ounces	245 grams
Honey, maple syrup, or corn syrup	1 tablespoon	0.75 ounce	20 grams
Liquids: cream, milk, water, or juice	1 cup	8 fluid ounces	240 milliliters
Salt	1 teaspoon	0.2 ounce	6 grams
Spices: cinnamon, cloves, ginger, or nutmeg (ground)	1 teaspoon	0.2 ounce	5 milliliters
Sugar, brown, firmly packed	1 cup	7 ounces	200 grams
Sugar, white	1 cup/1 tablespoon	7 ounces/0.5 ounce	200 grams/12.5 grams
Vanilla extract	1 teaspoon	0.2 ounce	4 grams

OVEN TEMPERATURES

Fahrenheit	Celsius	Gas Mark
225°	110°	¼
250°	120°	½
275°	140°	1
300°	150°	2
325°	160°	3
350°	180°	4
375°	190°	5
400°	200°	6
425°	220°	7
450°	230°	8

INDEX